# GONE TOO SOON

A Father's Journey Through Grief

Finding Strength, Love & Life
After Losing A Child

———————

Jonathan T. Baer

First Printing, 2013

ISBN 978-0-9891500-0-2

Library of Congress Control Number:  2013904774

IN MEMORY OF
Samantha Rose Baer

April 25, 2005 –  September 14, 2006

# CONTENTS

# FOREWORD

I first met Jon Baer in December, 2006 when he came to meet with me for his initial therapy appointment. Jon began the session by asking me about my experience helping people deal with the death of a loved one. I told Jon that in my 32 years as a therapist I have treated many clients who have lost loved ones, including parents whose children have died. I also told Jon that as an American Red Cross volunteer, I had gone to NY to meet with family members of those who had been killed in the 9/11 terrorist attack. I think it was important to Jon that he was not the first client I met with whose child had died. Jon proceeded to tell me about the death of Samantha, his 16 month-old daughter. As I listened to Jon's story, I felt strong emotions and struggled to maintain my own composure. The loss of a child is particularly difficult and, as a parent, I could not help but think about how I would feel if I suddenly lost my own son. I also remember being acutely aware of the sense of responsibility to be of help to this man who was in tremendous pain. That day was the beginning our 5 1/2 years of working together.

This is a book about grief, the sudden loss of a child, the challenges that men in particular face in grieving, and one man's personal experience in facing these challenges. Grief is the physical, emotional, and mental response we have to loss of any kind. Grieving means coming to accept what has happened in our life. Grief involves intense work. Grieving is often "two steps forward, and one step back". Events like anniversaries and holidays trigger recurrence of grief. Grief creates chaos, lives are turned upside down, and it can seem impossible to imagine getting on with living.

There are a number of psychological and sociological issues that make parental bereavement particularly difficult to resolve. Studies have found that the grief of parents is particularly severe when compared with other bereaved individuals. Parents who lose a child are multiply victimized. They are not only facing the loss of the child, but also the loss of the dreams and hopes invested in the child and the loss of their own self-esteem.

The impact of sudden death is an additional factor that overwhelms people and so severely reduces their functioning that recovery becomes all the more difficult. At least, when a death has been anticipated, there is some opportunity to prepare for the loss.

People grieve in many different ways. Through my years of experience in working with grieving individuals, I have found that men and women often grieve differently. In our society, many men find it difficult to express their personal feelings and needs. The elements of grieving, including sorrow, crying and the expression of emotion, seem to go against many of the typical traits we think of as being masculine, such as strength, pride, and toughness. Men tend to distrust their feelings. Many men worry that if they begin to let their feelings out, they will be unable to shut them off. Men are less likely to be comfortable with intimacy so friendships are often based on shared activities. While women often find the support they need from friends and family, men tend to grieve on the inside and often do not know where or how to get support. It is not surprising, therefore, that women are more likely than men to make use of therapy in response to a loss. Men are supposed to be strong, capable and in control. Talking to a mental health professional about their feelings may be associated with weakness and failure. As a result, men may feel very alone in their grief.

Although all bereaved people are somewhat socially stigmatized, parents whose children have died appear to report more of this than other mourners. They often experience abandonment, helplessness, and frustration when they are frequently avoided by other parents or believe they will be seen differently by other parents. As a result, many bereaved parents are left without many of the social and emotional supports desirable for coping with the grief process at the time when they are most in need of support.

One of the most difficult aspects of parental bereavement is that the death of the child strikes both spouses simultaneously and confronts them with the same overwhelming loss. Consequently, each partner's most important source of support is taken away as both are struggling with their own grief. Spouses are particularly vulnerable to the feelings of blame and anger that those grieving often displace onto those closest to them. Different grieving styles can strain the marital relationship. Spouses are often surprised to find that they do not experience the same grief even though they suffered the death of the same child. Each of them has had a unique relationship with their child.

This is a book about one man's personal experience of grieving for the loss of his daughter. Jon shares his efforts to cope with feeling a complete lack of control in his life and wondering if he would ever feel better. He writes about his initial tendency to isolate himself from friends, resenting their not knowing how to provide support, and discovering the importance of letting friends know how they can be supportive. Jon, who was initially reluctant to participate in therapy, take anti-depressant medication, or join a support group, shares his process of changing his mind and the benefits he found. He shares his struggle to accept the reality of his daughter's death and its impact on his faith. Jon writes about how to respond to the question, "How many children do you have?" and the challenges involved in deciding about having more children.

# LETTER TO MY DAUGHTER

## July 18, 2009

*Samantha,*

*Boy do I miss you. I can't even describe my longing for you. I wish I could hold you. I'd give anything to do so. It's like the earth has shattered beneath and around me. Everything has been turned upside down. Will anything ever be the same again? Will it always be like this for me?*

*Where are you now Samantha Rose? Can you see me? Can I hold you again? Can I ever feel you again?*

*Don't let me give up. I want to live and enjoy life. Can you help me with that? Please?*

*I am going to write a book, my love, on the journey we've taken since you died. It's for other daddies to help them cope.*

*Jake misses you.*

*Love,*

*Dad*

# ACKNOWLEDGEMENTS

There are many people whom I have to thank because without their support, I'm not sure I would have been able to successfully address my grief and "come out the other side" in one piece.

I want to thank my dear friends, especially the six guys who called me every week during the first year to check on me – Dan Silver, Barry Finegold, Steve Lubin, Joe Kershenbaum, Tom Powers, and Jon Sigel. These are guys who have their own busy lives and yet they always carved out time in their day to talk with me to make sure I was okay.

I also want to thank Jewish Family Services of Worcester for their involvement in my family's life. Steve Slaten, the executive director, deserves special credit because he introduced me to two very important people – Dave Hollis and Jody Sue Rutstein. Dave Hollis is my bereavement counselor, and I credit him with saving me and putting me on the road to recovery. Jody Sue Rutstein is the attorney who enabled us to adopt our precious Aiden.

Other people I want to thank include Rabbi Robert Goldstein, Jim Conviser, Steve Dame, Steve Branfman, Paul Paganelli, and David Domeshek and the rest of the guys at Fathers Forever, Tim Hawkins, Dean Dorazio, my Rat Gang buddies who insisted that I watch every Patriots game with them for the entire first year after Samantha passed (Brandon Bachner, Rich Mangano, Rob Retelle, Mike Epstein), Craig Nichols, Dan McGinn, and my editors Louise Aveni and Steve West. I need to thank Courtney Linehan, too, as she designed the book's front and back covers.

Another person I want to thank is Howard Stern. I don't know him, never met him, but when I watched his movie "Private Parts", the scene where he tells his wife Allison that the only way he's going to be successful is to not hold anything back resonated with me. When writing this book, I decided to take the same attitude. It was scary because I divulged some things I hadn't up to this point, so I want to thank Howard for inspiring me to tell the whole story when writing the book.

And then, of course, I want to thank my family; my wonderful and supportive wife Robin, my beautiful boys Jacob and Aiden, my parents, and my sister Andrea.

Robin was and continues to be, my rock. She's the one who kept the family together during the most difficult of times. She's the one who told Jake that Samantha had died and did it in such a beautiful, comforting way, by telling him that Samantha had gone up to heaven but she'd always look in on him to make sure he was alright. Robin kept me sane during my deepest moments of depression and, as I relate later in the book, it was Robin who encouraged me to stick with the golf league, which ended up being a real life saver for me. Without Robin's support, understanding and love, I'm not sure I would have progressed through the grieving process. I'm thankful for her!

I'm extremely appreciative for the support the whole community showered upon us. You're not going to believe this but for the first three months after Samantha died members of the community brought us dinner every night! Can you believe that? People who didn't even know us from a hole in the wall reached out with several groups within the town who took charge and organized the dinner delivery. As parents of young children themselves, I'm sure they could only imagine the pain we were in and assumed we'd be struggling to do the most simple of everyday tasks, such as cooking meals. So, in their generosity, they all chipped in and took turns making sure Jake, Robin and I ate a good dinner every night.

# INTRODUCTION:
## A STORY OF HOPE AND SURVIVAL

Our beloved Samantha suddenly and unexpectedly passed away on Thursday, September 14, 2006 at the age of 16 months. Her funeral was held the very next day. As I write this introduction to my first draft, it is July 2009, almost three years since her passing. Why did I wait so long to write this book? The answer is simple: it took me close to three years to finally feel human again. I'm still "not out of the woods" and as I state in many chapters of the book, having suffered the sudden loss of a child, life will never be the same again. However, at long last I'm at least able to talk about Samantha's passing in more depth and even briefly describe the circumstances surrounding her death. So, I'm ready...ready to share my story in the hope that it will provide others who will walk this same tragic road with some guidance to help them navigate through their own grieving process.

I'm just a regular guy who, prior to Samantha's death, had a pretty happy, normal, straightforward life. I enjoyed the classic two-parent, middle class suburban upbringing in a supportive, loving home, along with a younger sister and a dog. Happily, both my parents and sister are alive, and the only death I remember dealing with, prior to Samantha's death, was the passing of my grandparents and that of a high school friend, many years ago. Unlike my wife, Robin, who as a young child experienced the bitter divorce of her parents, I was never "tested;" so when Samantha unexpectedly passed away, I didn't have any tough experiences to fall back on to give me the confidence that I so desperately needed to survive this tragedy.

I chose to write this book as a real conversation between the reader and me, not only to make it easy to read but more importantly, to have the vignettes described in the book be completely relatable. I don't preach, tell you what to do, or argue that my way is the best and only way to move through the grieving process, because each one of us has to make our own decisions.

This is not a psychology book either, written by a medical or therapeutic professional who hasn't personally experienced what you and I have, nor is it an academic textbook on how to deal with grief. It's the true story of a dad who lost his baby girl way too early, and who does and always will miss her dearly.

This is a book that speaks directly to men who are dealing with the tragic loss of a child. I wrote this book primarily and specifically for men because, given my own experience, I witnessed how differently my wife handled herself after our loss. Like it or not, guys aren't wired to be touchy feely, or to call up a friend and cry on their shoulder. We're more likely to hold it in for fear of burdening our friends and appearing weak. Plus, we're not used to talking about this stuff. How many times have you had a conversation with your guy friends about how you're feeling? Now, compare that to the number of times you talked with your friends about last Sunday's football game or the last round of golf you played. We're simply more used to talking about the latter. Sharing our feelings, especially grief, is virgin territory for guys and just plain uncomfortable.

I also wrote this book for friends and loved ones of dads who have suffered the loss of a child. You may ask yourself, "What do I say to this guy?" or "What can I do to help?" or "I wonder how he's feeling and coping." This book is my attempt to answer those questions and can be used to as an aide in determining how best to help and support your friend or loved one suffering from this type of loss.

In many ways, I view this book as a blessing. It became a way for me to look back on the decisions I made and on the situations I had to deal with and how I persevered through them all and now I can proudly say to myself "job well done!"

It provided me with an unlooked for opportunity to pat myself on the back for getting through the most difficult times following Samantha's passing and for having the courage to live life connected, rather than remain numb and have it pass me by. I'm proud of myself for those decisions and for the healthier path I chose. Believe me, it was brutal, and it's still not over. You never get over the loss of a child. You adapt. Now I want to share my story with you in the hope of helping you successfully pass through the multi- stages of your own grieving.

There's no playbook on how to deal with the loss of a child. Nothing can prepare you for such a loss and the devastating emotions that follow. How am I going to deal with this? How do I get through it? Can I get through it? These are all questions I struggled with and I'm sure you're grappling with them now, too.

It is my hope that this book provides you with thoughts and ideas to consider in an effort to help you cope with your loss and provide aid in formulating your own game plan as you navigate this painful journey. Everyone is different, but I think the experiences I share in this book, while unique to me, will in some way, assist you in yours. Hopefully, you'll come away with tools that will ease your grief, even if it's as simple as saying to yourself, "This guy got through it. I can too!"

# THE INITIAL EFFECTS

# THE UNTHINKABLE HAPPENS

Around 7:30, on the night of September 13th, 2006, my wife, Robin, and I were getting Samantha ready for bed. She seemed fine, a normal 16-month-old girl. In fact, she was dancing around her room before we tucked her into bed and kissed her goodnight. Sometime later she began crying, so we went to her room to see what the problem was, only to find that she was hot with fever. We reacted as any parents would. We comforted her. We tried to cool her down with wet cloths, without success. When she began having difficulty breathing, we realized she needed medical attention as quickly as possible, so we rushed her to the emergency room at a nearby hospital.

To our shock and horror, she was put on life support and by 12:30 a.m. that very night, everything ceased. We told the doctors to pull the plug. Our lives were forever changed by a viral nuclear bomb that had hit her little body without warning. Our Samantha was gone!

-    -    -

We planned her funeral the next day. I sat in the living room with my wife Robin, our son Jake, my sister and my parents. We were talking with the funeral director about details and logistics, things that had to be decided and taken care of, but that I couldn't think about. I was going through the motions. When that conversation was over, my father turned to me and told me I looked like I had just gone through a street fight… and lost. My eyes were red and swollen from crying and I was walking around dazed and disconnected.

My mother, obviously very concerned about me, took me into the kitchen, away from everyone else, and said to me, "Jake has such a beautiful smile. You have a responsibility to him to continue to be a father to him so that he doesn't change. If he loses that precious smile, it'll be a double tragedy."

My immediate reaction was one of anger. I said, "What about me? I'm hurting too! I don't know how I'm going to take care of myself, let alone Jake and Robin." Not wanting to argue with me, she walked away, while I remained in the kitchen looking at everyone congregating in the living room. Jake, who was a little over three years old at the time, was smiling as he played with my sister. I'm sure he knew something was amiss, yet he still had that precious, innocent, ear-to-ear, contagious smile of his. The realization that my mother was right suddenly hit me squarely in the face. Look at that innocent little child, I thought. He's just a kid. Don't let this tragedy cause him to lose his innocence, his outgoing and happy personality. She's right! I needed to be there for Jake because he wants and deserves to have a dad who's involved in his life. It's not fair to make him yet another victim of this tragedy.

- - -

If I didn't want Jake to lose his smile, then I had to be sure that I didn't lose mine. I decided to adopt my mother's advice, "Don't Lose Your Smile," as my mantra. It was that simple phrase, repeated again and again to myself, that kept me going during those initial very dark and painful months following Samantha's death. Whenever I felt especially depressed or started thinking about how much easier it would be to either hit the bottle or end my own life--and yes, those thoughts will come--I'd remember what my mother said and I would repeat it several times. Don't lose your smile. Then I would picture Jake's beautiful, innocent, joyous smile. Believe it or not, as simple as this seems, it got me through some of my darkest days. It was a mental exercise that reminded me of, and reinforced, my responsibility to Jake. It gave me the strength to make some very tough decisions about how to live life after suffering such heartbreak.

But there's also another meaning to the phrase, a meaning that's important for myself, and for you. At the time Samantha passed away I was 40 years old, so my own life was barely half over. I still had many years ahead of me. One of the most important decisions you'll ever have to make is how you will respond to your loss.

Will you decide to live life as an active participant, enjoying it as much as you can despite your loss? Or will you let your grief overwhelm you and dictate how to live out the rest of your years? Will you choose to lose your smile, give up on life and retreat into a cocoon? I know several men who decided to take that exact route; their marriages failed, their career paths derailed, and they've been miserable for years.

It happened with former Red Sox pitcher, Jeff Reardon. According to Wikipedia, he's currently ranked seventh on the all-time Major League Baseball saves list with 367. His sad story, as mentioned in Wikipedia, culminated in an embarrassing arrest for armed robbery for the former pitcher. According to Wikipedia, he was ultimately found not guilty of the charges by reason of insanity. It may seem hard to believe that a person with the mental strength and discipline of a professional athlete, who was named to the All Star team four times in his career, could unravel like that. But having been through the same loss and anguish, I now understand how it can happen. It doesn't have to happen, however. I had a choice, just as you have a choice. You must make the decision now, as early as you can in your grief, that you will take a different path. You must find a way to smile.

If you are still in the early days of dealing with your loss, then you may react as I did. How could my mother talk to me about smiling when I had lost so much? I urge you to take some time and think about how profound and important her advice was to me, and can be to you. My mother was wise enough to recognize that importance, and loving enough--for all of our family--to make me hear it. It was the first piece of advice she gave me at that worst time of my life, and she was right. I pass her advice on to you, and hope it can help you too.

# ANXIETY HITS HARD

It came at me almost immediately after Samantha passed away, an overwhelming onslaught of anxiety. My bereavement counselor called it "post traumatic stress disorder." Besides the shock from her sudden death, the realization that I had no control over anything caused me to spin out of control myself. One moment Samantha was happily dancing in her room, a healthy, normal, little girl just having some fun before bedtime, the next moment we were telling the doctors to cease all life support. Talk about loss of control!

The anxiety I felt was like nothing I had experienced before. I'm talking about heart-pounding, sweaty palms, frozen in your spot, "Oh my god, I can't breathe!" anxiety. The kind that explodes without warning and hits so hard you're sure you're going to lose your mind. And it only gets worse, because once you start believing you *are* losing your mind, you wonder whether you'll ever find your way back and return to some sense of normalcy. What can scare you even more is the thought that you might *never* return, spending the rest of your life lost in a mental abyss.

You may be familiar with the famous painting "The Scream" by Edvard Munch. To me, the painting represents a man who's completely overwhelmed, riddled with anxiety and unable to handle it anymore, so he screams out in anguish. That's how I felt for a very long time after Samantha passed away, precariously hanging onto sanity by a thread.

One night in those first few months, I was awakened by the sound of Jake coughing in his room. It was a horrible, hacking sound, like a long-term smoker's cough. Given my precarious mental state, my first thought was, *He's going to die!*

My heart began pounding uncontrollably. I was sweating profusely and gasping for air. My whole body was shaking. I got out of bed and started to make my way towards his bedroom, but my legs felt as if I were walking through quicksand. My mind kept commanding me, *Call 911! Jake is going to die. Don't make the same mistake again. Don't let Jake die!*

By the time Robin and I got to his room, he was breathing heavily and still coughing. Fortunately, my wife stayed calm, unlike me, and quickly gave Jake his inhaler. You see, Jake has asthma and that was why he was coughing. But I had forgotten all that in my anxiety and panic. I truly thought he was going to die.

When I relayed the story a few weeks later to my family doctor he said, "Jon. A cough is just a cough." Intellectually, I knew he was right. Jake wasn't going to die from a cough, but having been completely traumatized by Samantha's death, in my damaged mind, a cough was a prelude to death. The suddenness of Samantha's passing, accompanied by the complete lack of control over the circumstances, made it impossible for me to comprehend that a cough is a just a cough.

The fact is, anxiety can literally make you crazy, and if you let it run amok without working to hold it in check, you'll find it virtually impossible to recover from your loss.

I made the anxiety worse in those early months by reliving, in my mind, Samantha's last moments of life, as if I could somehow hold onto her that way. It was unbearable to think about and yet, for a long time, I couldn't help going there. I was drawn to that memory as if it were some type of emotional magnet. I knew what I was doing was not healthy. Samantha was dead, and going back to that scene again and again would never change anything. And besides, I needed to move on. Replaying that scene only kept me stuck in that moment, making my anxiety worse and preventing me from letting go. And yet, I kept returning.

-   -   -

Two years later, I was still struggling with this problem. I had trouble holding my focus on anything for very long. When I played golf in my league, my thoughts wandered aimlessly throughout the entire round. This was especially true when my partner and I would split off, his ball going to the right and mine to the left. Instead of concentrating on the shot at hand, I'd start thinking about Samantha, the good times we had together, how much I missed her and then, of course, the ultimate end. I worried about whether or not I might I freak out and lose my mind on the course.

Despite all the time that had passed, I still had not developed the mental fortitude to pull my thoughts out of that dark place and back to the present. I would become withdrawn and depressed and, as a result, I was bad at golf and bad company as well. And when the round was over, I would wave off the customary round of beer with the guys and head straight for home.

Because this happened more than half the time, my anxiety about playing golf increased in frequency as well as intensity. While I looked forward to getting out onto the golf course, at the same time I was incredibly apprehensive. *Would it happen again? Would I fall apart on the course, in front of my friends?* What should have been an enjoyable afternoon would often turn out to be a nerve-wracking experience. Even a game I loved had become consumed and almost ruined by my anxiety.

The point I want to make is this: anxiety can have a life of its own, and when it decides to rear its nasty head, it will hit you hard! There's no conceivable way the human body can absorb a loss of this magnitude without serious repercussion. So, in no way should you be hard on yourself, or think that you're weak for allowing this anxiety to overtake you.

I'm not saying you need to get used to the feeling, or that it will be with you for the rest of your life. All I'm saying is that it's a natural occurrence, and so you will have to come to terms with it and develop a game plan on how you intend to deal with it.

In my case, whenever my mind went to Samantha's last moments of life, I learned to make a concentrated, conscious effort to pivot my thinking and get out of that mindset as fast as possible. You know how when you touch something really hot, you instinctively pull your hand away? I tried to do the same thing whenever my mind got too hot with those tragic thoughts. I realized that if I stayed there, I would only get burned, and I would simply be feeding my unhappiness and anxieties for a very long time.

It was not easy, and I had to work at it. But now, as I write this, it has been almost three years since Samantha's passing and I can confidently state that I'm able to pull myself "back from the brink" without much effort at all. Whenever my mind begins to wander to a place that's not healthy, I'm instantly able to recognize it and say to myself, *Stop! Going there isn't good for you. Get back to the present. You're here to enjoy your round and the company of your buddies. Don't go down that path because if you do, you'll get bummed out, have a lousy round and go back into your cocoon.* I finally have the self-belief that I can stop these negative, unhealthy thoughts, and redirect them to a much healthier place.

Sadness and depression may never go away completely and all the time. How could it? But you can reach a point where these feelings do not control and overwhelm you. Instead, you can gain control of your thoughts and your memories. Then there will come a day when you'll be able to choose when and how you want to reminisce about your child, both in life and in death. And as you regain your emotional strength, your mind will no longer go to the end--unless *you* decide to go there.

# THE SCARLET LETTER EFFECT

I remember reading "The Scarlet Letter," by Nathaniel Hawthorne, in high school. It's the story of a married woman who had an affair in Puritan Boston in the 1640s. As punishment for her sin, she was ordered to wear a big scarlet "A" on her clothing, signifying to the entire community that she had committed adultery. Everywhere she went, people knew what she had done.

With Samantha's death, I too felt as if I carried a designation that everyone could see. It was as if I had a bright spotlight shining on my back, or a neon sign that flashed, "I'm the guy whose kid tragically died recently." It was a weird feeling, but a very real effect, as real as if I actually did have a scarlet letter on my clothes. No matter where I went, I was sure that people were staring at me and whispering behind my back. "Psst," I imagined them saying, "that's the guy who just lost his kid. Tread lightly around him." There were times when this impression felt so intense that I would actually start sweating, and I could feel my back getting hotter and hotter. I came to call it the Scarlet Letter Effect.

Not only did this effect cause me to experience extreme anxiety and paranoia, it eventually forced me to withdraw from social events and avoid everyday experiences. I would even avoid going to the grocery store during busy hours for fear someone I knew would start asking questions or feel compelled to extend their sympathy.

Whenever my golfing buddies asked me to meet them for a drink or our friends invited us to parties, I simply couldn't bring myself to go. I dreaded the typical questions that new people I met would be asking, like "How many kids do you have?" or "How old are your kids?" Normal questions for most people, but for a father who had just lost a child, the thought of having to come up with an answer, any answer, immobilized me completely.

I clearly remember the first time I was rocked by the Scarlet Letter Effect. Robin and I had been invited to a party about a month after Samantha's death. The party was hosted by a good friend of ours and we knew most of the attendees. As soon as I walked into the room, I immediately felt that imaginary bright spotlight on my back, announcing to everyone, "Here's that guy who lost his kid." The feeling was so powerful that it set off a chemical chain reaction that instantly brought on the sweats. I could barely talk to my friends. And when I looked into their eyes, I *swear* I could hear their thoughts: "Your kid just died. I can't begin to imagine how you're feeling. What are you doing at a party, anyway?" It was all I could think about. I was completely helpless and couldn't stop the nonsense that was swirling around in my head. I convinced myself that I could feel their pity for me, engulfing not only me but the entire room.

It was probably true that many people had such thoughts. But it's also true that I let myself get completely carried away by the feeling that everyone was talking about me, thinking about me, and pitying me.

Here's another example. Around Thanksgiving, about two and a half months after Samantha died, I was invited to hook up with some of my golf league buddies at a bar, along with a bunch of other guys from town. I didn't want to go. In fact, seeing all these guys for the first time after Samantha's death scared the heck out of me! *Would they talk about her death? Could I handle it? What if I started to cry?* I decided, *The heck with it! I'm not going. Too much stress. I'll just stay home and have a few beers by myself.*

As it happened, my parents were at the house that night and when I announced that I'd chosen to stay home, it was my father who took me aside this time and said, "You *have* to go. You need to get out of the house. You need to socialize. You can't live in this cocoon for the rest of your life. It's not healthy. You're not getting any better. Going out, being around the guys, having a few beers and a few laughs will do you a world of good. Please go." So I went.

When I pulled into the parking lot and saw my buddies' cars, my hands started shaking. I'm not kidding. I was scared out of my mind! All I could think about was, *These guys are going to see me and the first thing they're going to say is, "What's he doing here? He just lost his daughter."*

And as if that weren't enough, I began to obsess over what my friends would say to the guys who didn't know me. "See that guy who just walked in? Be nice to him because his daughter recently died." So, I sat in the car and tried to muster the courage to go in. *Will I freak out? Should I just go home?* Normally, I'd be excited to see the guys, but these insecure thoughts were brand new to me and, quite honestly, scared the heck out of me. I simply couldn't control it.

I considered sitting in the car for thirty minutes or so and then heading home, where I could just tell everyone what a wonderful time I had. But I decided I couldn't do that. For one, I'd made a promise to my father. And besides, he was right, it *would* be good for me. It would be the first time I'd socialized since the party where the Scarlet Letter Effect had hit me for the first time.

Finally I gathered my nerve and walked into the crowded bar. I was greeted by a mass of people who seemed to be staring at me and appeared genuinely surprised to see me there. I tried joining a group of guys who were standing around talking, but I didn't have the energy to join the conversation, so I just stood there like a bump on a log. This was totally alien to me, being an observer rather than a participant.

I wondered if it was the conversation itself that was making it difficult for me to join in, and so I tried engaging in conversation with yet another group of guys, but the exact same thing happened again. I thought, *Welcome to the new Jon. The quiet, introspective guy who doesn't have the energy or desire to talk to people.* It was no use, I just couldn't relate to these guys. Here they were, excited to be hanging out, having a few beers with one another, laughing and having a great time. But not me. I was miserable!

I think I lasted a total of about fifteen minutes and then ran out so fast, I didn't even take the time to say "goodbye," let alone "hello," to most of them.

When I arrived home, I couldn't lie and so I told everyone what had happened. While disappointed that I didn't stay longer, my father and Robin said they fully understood where I was coming from and felt badly for me. They so wanted me to have a good time; to smile for once. I simply wasn't ready to hold a light-hearted conversation with anyone. It was too soon. I was way too self-absorbed in my misery.

For the most part, I found it easier if I simply stopped going out socially. I went to work and then came home, and that was it in terms of any socializing or interacting with others. I even stopped returning phone calls and, unfortunately, lost touch with some of my closest friends. For the time being, I simply refused to allow myself to enter into situations where I might have to deal with any uncomfortable questions, as I simply couldn't handle it.

Meanwhile, the chatter in my head continued. *What if so and so asks me about Samantha? What if I start crying during the conversation? Do I want to burden this person with my pain? How will they react if I tell them?* Ultimately, I decided this was too much stress. I was just going to stop talking to friends because the whole thing was too painful and nerve wracking for me.

All the everyday social activities that used to be routine became anxiety provoking. It got so bad, I stopped going to the bank because I knew all the tellers and feared that they'd ask me how I was doing. I even hated going to birthday parties thrown by the parents of Jake's friends because all those families had kids around Jake's and Samantha's ages. And yet another casualty to our social interaction was that Robin, Jake and I stopped going to our favorite restaurant. I just couldn't face having to relive the story of Samantha's death to the owner, whom we had gotten to know.

-   -   -

These vignettes are only a few examples of how my anxiety problem multiplied and grew from a "mole hill" into a "mountain." Perhaps it won't hit you in quite the same way that it hit me, but I'm sure most men will feel something like it.

So what's the best way to get over this anxiety when it comes to social settings? First, you need to accept the fact that people just don't know what to say. They really don't. What do you say to a guy who just lost his kid? "I'm sorry," while politically correct, may sound too trivial. And yet, as you look into their eyes and see the sadness reflected back, maybe that's their way of telling you, "I feel your pain. I hurt, too, when I think about your loss."

The second way to overcome this anxiety is to ask for support. This is something most men are not good at. Whether it's in our DNA or the way we are raised, it's not in our nature to ask for help. So don't think of it as asking for help. Think of it as taking control, because that's what it really is.

You know how good it feels when a friend reaches out and says, "I'm thinking about you. How are you doing?" You savor the strength you feel emerging when you realize that there are others out there pulling for you. If you're completely honest with yourself, you know you want your friends to ask about you, to offer comfort and help. So why not come right out and say, "I need to know you're pulling for me. Please reach out every once in a while." And let me tell you, when you do, I guarantee your friend will deliver in spades. Trust me.

What an empowering moment it is for both of you when you say to him, "I need your help." Not only does it free you from the fear of rejection, but it also provides your friend the permission he needs to do what he's wanted to do all along, which is to help you through this horrible period. All along, he's probably been saying to himself "I know my friend is hurting, but if I say something, that'll just make him feel worse, won't it?"

I believe that guys really do want to help, but because men are trained to "tough it out," and "deal with it," and "work it out on your own," they just don't know how to get started. That's why I'm suggesting that you help them to help you, by telling them what you need in terms of support. If you want them to check in with you, then tell them. Give them permission, and doing so will not only make them feel better, it will also benefit you by providing a sense of being in control.

Last, but certainly not least, if there are topics that are "off limits," say so. Let them know the boundaries. How are they supposed to help you if you don't guide them and give them directions? Remember – don't get mad. Some people, particularly men, aren't intuitively astute about such things, but that doesn't mean they don't want to be. Show them the way.

For me, taking these actions seemed to reduce, if not eliminate, The Scarlet Letter Effect entirely. The people I had been afraid to face became instead the very people who could help me, and did. Which is what we all wanted all along.

# THE HEAVY WET BLANKET

Before Samantha's passing, I had never experienced severe depression. Sure, there were times when I'd get bummed out just like everyone else, but never to the point of deep depression. In fact, I was one of those people who, when hearing that someone was depressed, would say to myself, *They need to get over it* or *Just deal with it.* It's not that I'm unsympathetic, I just plain didn't understand how depression could cause such a chemical imbalance in the brain, resulting in the creation of an emotional behavior beyond one's control.

All of that changed with Samantha's death, which triggered in me the type of depression I had never understood before. I labeled my bouts of depression "The Heavy Wet Blanket" because when they hit, they felt like someone had placed an extremely heavy, soaking wet blanket over my shoulders. The feeling was similar to those weighted vests you wear when having an x-ray taken, only multiplied a hundred-fold. It wasn't just a mental state, it was a physical sensation and it weighed me down.

These episodes could last a day or run for several weeks at a time, and this unpredictability was the most unnerving thing about it. At least when I caught a cold or the flu, I expected and accepted the fact that I'd probably feel lousy for a week or so, but I knew eventually the feeling would go away. Not so with the Heavy Wet Blanket. When the experience came on, coupled with extreme anxiety, I had no idea how long it would last.

It wasn't just feeling intense sadness; it went so much deeper than that. I felt as if the whole world had come crushing down upon me. The depression ran so deep into my core that I couldn't conceive how it could possibly get any worse... and yet it did. Time and again, just when I thought I'd reached the bottom, the floor fell out from underneath me and I would fall even further. It was terrifying and it literally sucked the life out of me. *Will this ever end? Am I going to be feeling this way for the rest of my life? What if it gets worse? Will I be able to handle it?*

I was a complete mess after the first few rounds of the Heavy Wet Blanket, mostly because I was totally unprepared for them, and I was clueless about how to cope with the barrage of random emotions that engulfed me.

The episodes always began with a physical pain in my gut, as if someone punched me in the stomach, only much worse, because it stayed and radiated throughout my entire body. When the initial ache would finally subside after several minutes, that's when I'd get hit with anxiety. This combination of the internal, gut wrenching cauldron of nerves, coupled with the weight of the world on my shoulders, was sometimes more than I could bear. My shoulders would literally begin to bend and curve inward from the weight I was carrying. And I carried it for a long time.

-　-　-

The Heavy Wet Blanket could descend on me at any moment.

One night, about a year or so after Samantha died, Jake was dancing to some music that was playing in his room. It was great just watching him. Robin and I smiled from ear to ear and were grateful for the much needed respite from all the sadness we'd both been feeling for so long. Jake was having a heck of a time, as his mother and I clapped and laughed along with him. When he finally stopped I asked him how he had learned to dance so well and his answer rocked me to my core. "Samantha taught me" he said.

That simple answer deflated me as quickly as a popped balloon. It was an instant 180-degree reversal of emotions, from feeling happy to utterly devastated. I fell into a deep hole that took weeks to dig out of.

Not even a kiss or hug from my Jake could alleviate the depression I felt during a Heavy Wet Blanket episode. Everything was a struggle and everyday tasks became a hassle. Just getting out of bed in the morning took an enormous amount of effort. My limbs felt like they had lead weights attached to them. It took a monumental struggle just to lift my feet off the ground and place one foot in front of the other. As it turned out, sleep was my only escape from the unpredictable and unwanted episodes.

I don't mind admitting, I was tough to be around during this time. Jake would say, "Dad…want to play with my trucks and cars?" To which I'd answer, "Not now Jake. Daddy's not feeling well." Robin would often ask, "Want to go out to dinner with so and so?" To which I'd reply, "No. It's too much of a hassle. I don't want to deal with being friendly and engaging in small talk." And it even carried into my work environment. Most of the time, I was just plain grumpy and miserable.

As time passed, I came to accept the Heavy Wet Blanket episodes as a natural by-product of our tragedy, and I learned how to cope with them when they paid me an unwelcomed visit. I chose not to fight them, even though I could see them coming. Sort of like knowing when a train is approaching; while you might not see it coming, the vibrations on the ground announce its imminent arrival. Once I recognized the warnings that an episode was on the way, I only had to remind myself that I had successfully dealt with them the last time, and this time would be no different. I knew they would go away eventually, and that's what I hung onto.

After about a dozen occurrences, I finally gained the confidence to know that I could handle the episodes whenever they arrived. They usually came in waves. Sometimes, I'd go days, weeks, or even months without experiencing them and then, all of a sudden, something innocent would trigger an event, such as seeing a family happily pushing their baby in a stroller, or going to a birthday party and seeing siblings enjoying playing with one another. As I got more accustomed to the causes and effects of the episodes, I learned to deal with them.

In an effort to stave off the rampant anxiety that often accompanied the Heavy Wet Blanket, I'd give myself a pep talk, saying things like, *Just accept it. Deal with it. Let it run its course. It'll be over soon.* In other words, I was determined to neither fight them nor fear them. I simply accepted all that as part of my grieving process. My attitude shifted to *since there's nothing I can do about it, why get all anxious about it?* It became my new reality. In fact, I remember one time my mother asked me about these episodes and my only answer was, "It is what it is."

- - -

Now, at the third anniversary of Samantha's death, I'm happy to report that it has been a long time since the Heavy Wet Blanket has appeared. In fact, it didn't even hit me this anniversary at all. Sure, I was deeply saddened in the weeks leading up to it, and naturally on the actual day, but the great news is that I didn't turn into a complete basket case.

Why? I really don't know. That old saying, "Time heals all wounds," may be the reason. Perhaps it's due to the fact that the intensity of the feelings of loss has softened or maybe it's due to the work I've been doing with my bereavement counselor. Whatever the reason, all I can say is thank goodness the Heavy Wet Blanket no longer seems to be part of my existence. Even if it does return, I'm now better prepared to handle it because I know it's only a temporary condition and I realize that no matter how bad it gets, I'll persevere.

So, here's the lesson I hope you take away from this chapter: recognize that severe depression can be a normal aftershock from what you've been through, that you're not losing your mind, and most importantly, that you're not alone.

Every guy who has ever lost a child will experience his own version of the Heavy Wet Blanket, so take comfort in knowing you're not the only man who feels this way. As a matter of fact, if you don't feel horribly depressed after the death of your child, you've got an even bigger issue.

Remember the responsibilities you have, not only to others but to yourself, for it is your birthright to live life as best you can. Try not to get down on yourself when you stumble, but try instead to give yourself credit when something goes well, and indulge yourself with a frequent "pat on the back" for a job well done. The complete package of life is to be an active participant, rather than a passive observer; to be a parent who is present in your surviving children's life; to remain an engaged partner and friend to your spouse. Continue your interactions with your coworkers because you're a member of the same team; and be mindful of your friends and extended family and don't let this loss ruin those paramount relationships you've built up through the years.

For me at least, focusing on these responsibilities was one of the best tactics I used to combat, and finally defeat, the Heavy Wet Blanket.

# PICTURE PAIN

Photos of our children line the stairway leading up to our bedrooms on the second floor of our house. I pass these photos first thing in the morning when I go downstairs for breakfast, and then again on my way up to bed at the end of the day.

Jake's collage appears first on the way up the stairs, because he's the oldest, and then Samantha's is right after his. Directly across from the landing, at the bottom of the stairs, we have a big picture of Samantha wearing a party dress and displaying one of those precious, smirking smiles that perfectly captures her sweet, adorable, happy, little-girl personality. That's the photo I see every morning as I walk down the stairs-- if and when I choose to look up at it, that is.

For the first couple of years after Samantha's death, I couldn't bear to look at those pictures of her. Seeing them only tore me apart and left me feeling emotionally drained, a reaction that would linger for a long time. So I began walking up and down that stairway with my eyes closed.

I've always kept photos of my family on my desk at work, some in frames and some lying loose where I can look through them at any time. One day, not long after Samantha passed away, one of my colleagues took one of the unframed photos of her to the store and bought a beautiful picture frame for it. When I returned from lunch, there it was – a photo of Samantha taken on her first birthday, about four months prior to her death. She looked like a little angel in that photo. It's one of my favorites, and also one of the most painful to look at.

Within a few days, I began to feel incredibly depressed and sad. I experienced a resurgence of my anxiety, and I was finding it extremely difficult to focus on my job. At first, I couldn't figure out why I was feeling this way. What had changed to cause these emotions to rise up unexpectedly? Of course, the answer was right in front of me: Samantha's photo! Instead of lifting me up and filling my mind and heart with happy, soothing memories of her and that wonderful birthday, it did the complete opposite. It simply ruined me.

So, I took the photo, turned it upside down and stuck it in one of my desk drawers. I still have difficulty looking at it for long periods of time, but at least now I can take an occasional quick glance, which I consider progress.

Another photo that still troubles me, and yet I feel drawn to every so often, was taken approximately two weeks before Samantha's death. It shows her in the parking lot of an animal petting zoo that we used to visit. She's sitting in her stroller and I'm kneeling down with my arm around it. She's beaming the most beautiful, innocent smile that says it all: "I'm so excited. I'm here with my family. My Daddy loves me and I love him. Life is great."

In this shot, I'm wearing a T-shirt I purchased while on a trip to Bermuda and, in fact, I still have that shirt today. But for a long time I couldn't wear it because it reminded me of that day. I was afraid that putting it on would bring back the memories and throw me into a deep funk for days. Yet I didn't want to throw it out either because somehow that would represent trying to forget about Samantha, which certainly was not what I wanted either. So the shirt sat in my drawer, a small but constant reminder of what I could, and could not, handle.

Finally, after almost three years, one day I was able to put it on, and boy, did it feel great! I proudly proclaimed to my wife, "Look! I'm wearing the T-shirt." She smiled at me and said "Congratulations!" which felt tremendous because we both knew that wearing this shirt was another triumph, another example that I was healing emotionally. I know this all sounds crazy. After all, it's just a T-shirt for crying out loud! But to me it was a small victory in my ever-evolving grieving process.

-    -    -

I have to admit, I used to feel guilty about not looking at Samantha's photos. Was I being disrespectful of her? Was I trying to put her and my memories of her out of my life? The last thing I wanted to do was turn that old adage, "out of sight – out of mind," into reality for my Samantha. I talked about this struggle at length with my bereavement counselor, and eventually I came to understand that looking or not looking at the photos actually had nothing to do with Samantha. It was all about me and my ability to successfully advance through the grieving process. Whatever worked best for me, and helped me to handle my grief, was the right thing to do.

As time passed and I grew even more determined to push through the grieving process, I found the strength to start looking at the photos again. Sometimes a glance, sometimes more, I would look at the photos as I came down the stairs. Now, on occasion, I can even give one or two of the pictures a kiss and say, "Hi baby. I miss you. I hope you're doing well wherever you are." However, I'm still not able to put photos of Samantha on my desk. That would be too much "in my face." For the time being, her photos stay in the drawer, waiting patiently for the day when I am ready to pull them out again.

-    -    -

Pictures have power. It's why we take them, and why we save them, as reminders of those we love and the experiences we have shared. For the father who has lost a child, that power becomes a double-edged sword. You want to remember, but do you dare? Dealing with this conflict is a challenge you will have to face on your own terms. I can only offer this advice: don't feel guilty if you can't look at photos of your lost child. You will probably have to go through a transition, possibly a long one, from considering these photos as only a horrible reminder of your loss, to a time when you can choose to embrace them as a comforting pathway that allows you to relive those wonderful moments with your child.

The one thing I haven't done yet, and quite frankly, I don't know if or when I'll *ever* be able to, is to watch the hours of video tapes I have of her. For now, all the tapes are safely locked in a fireproof safe because they're invaluable to me and just plain irreplaceable. Someday, perhaps when Jake is older and he wants to remember what his baby sister was like, I'll pull them out and we can watch them together. Someday.

Related to the photo phobia was another challenge I had for the longest time. I had great difficulty looking at other little girls, especially ones around Samantha's age at the time she died, or at the age she would have been had she still been alive.

I recall one incident in particular, when I was standing next to a good friend of ours who was holding her 12-month old daughter. While we were having a nice conversation, I couldn't bring myself to look at my friend *or* her baby. Instead, I alternated between putting my hand on the side of my face (like a blinder on a horse) and turning my back to her. I must have appeared rude and looked like a complete idiot to anyone watching, but I was helpless to do anything about it. I could either behave as I did, or walk to the other side of the room and not speak with my friend at all. Fortunately for me, she was very understanding and didn't take offense at my odd behavior.

Over time, I found my comfort level and I was able to at least look at girl toddlers from a distance, but I continued to experience difficulty being in the same room with them and would eventually have to leave.

About two years after Samantha's death, I knew I had successfully progressed through this challenge when I actually played with that same little girl on whom I had turned my back a year before. I was in our living room playing with Jake and his friend, throwing them onto our big, comfortable couch, while the friend's little sister hung out in the kitchen with her parents. The two boys laughed their heads off, and provided me with a great workout lifting them up. Everyone was having a lot of fun.

When the boys took a break and went into the kitchen to get something to drink, I sat down on the couch to catch my breath. Not thirty seconds later, in walks the friend's little sister. Because I had my eyes closed, I hadn't seen her enter, but all of a sudden I felt her poking at me. As soon as I opened my eyes, there before me was this sweet little girl with a huge smile on her face. She couldn't really talk at the time, but clearly indicated to me that she wanted to be tossed onto the couch, just like the older boys had been. At first I said, "I'm sorry, but I can't. I can't hold little girls," which was a pretty unfair statement to make to a two year old. She started crying, and so I felt obligated to pick her up and gently place her on the couch; a tamed-down version of what I had been doing with the boys. At first it didn't feel right, picking up someone else's little girl. You see, I had made a promise of sorts to Samantha, whereby I told her I wouldn't pick up or kiss another little girl unless it was my own. But as we kept playing, she was laughing and having a ball, and the truth of the matter was, so was I. After a couple of minutes, *I* was the one who didn't want the game to stop. Picking up this little girl and seeing her laugh so freely made me feel terrific. It brought me back to happier days when I used to play with Samantha like that.

While we played in the living room, I overheard the grownups in the kitchen whisper, "*Hurry up and look at Jon. Look who he's playing with.*" Out of the corner of my eye, I could see them craning their necks to watch me play with her. They were smiling from ear to ear and I sensed their joy in seeing how much progress I'd made.

When we were done playing, I gave myself a major pat on the back and for several days after, I couldn't stop bragging to my wife about it. I was just as ecstatic to share this with my bereavement counselor, my parents and my sister, as it marked a triumphant win for me and one more solid step forward in the grieving process.

Jake's friend's little sister is four years old now, and we play together all the time. But I still refrain from hugging or kissing her, which makes me feel bad because she's indicated that she'd like to give me a kiss--and get one from me. I'm confident that someday, when I'm ready, I will be able to give her that kiss.

# THE THOUGHT OF MY OWN DEATH BRINGS COMFORT

Before Samantha passed away, I can honestly say that I was afraid to die. Oh, I accepted that it was going to happen eventually, but I dreaded the inevitability of it all. Perhaps it was because I had never had to deal with the death of a very close loved one before. Often, when you don't fully understand something, it becomes pretty darn intimidating, even frightening.

When I was in college, during winter and summer breaks, I did some volunteer work for the Samaritans, a suicide prevention hotline. I signed up because one of my high school teacher's sons had committed suicide. I witnessed, firsthand, how this boy's death had devastated his mother and wanted to do whatever I could to prevent this from happening to any other family.

At that time in my life, I simply couldn't understand how or why someone would want to take his or her own life. *Why can't these people just get over it?* I often wondered. *Why is it so bad that they feel their only option is suicide? Are things really that painful?*

After Samantha died, I was finally able to understand that kind of pain. I felt how horrific that level of depression was and how taxing it could be on your psyche and nervous system, indeed on your entire body and soul. Worst of all, I found that this kind of depression was unrelenting; it never let up. Just when I thought it couldn't get any worse or the depression couldn't get any deeper, I'd experience a devastating blow of one type or another, spinning me out of control yet again. I just couldn't catch a break.

There were days, especially in the first year after Samantha's death, that I would have given anything to stop the pain. It was a pain that entrenched itself deep in my core. I could actually *feel* it in every fiber of my being, and each time I took a breath. The pain was unbearable. I battled a constant, unforgiving and never-ending depression and anxiety.

During some of my darkest days, when the depression overrode my sanity, it took me to some very scary, unimaginable places, ones I didn't know existed. I actually pictured myself dead and thought, *I'm coming to see you, honey. I can't wait to hold you in my arms again, see your smile, hear you laugh and feel you pat me on the back.*

In a weird way, these visions made me feel a little bit better, because death, even imagined, offered a relief from the pain and anguish. Death was literally the "light at the end of the tunnel" and meant that I could be with Samantha once again and feel some joy, an infrequent emotion that I sorely missed. Essentially, I was convinced that I'd find more comfort in death than in life.

Like anyone else who's experienced this type of loss, I certainly expected to feel depressed. I wasn't kidding myself. But thoughts this dark? This was unchartered territory for me. When I went there, I would often ask myself, *What in the world are you thinking? Why are you doing this?* This self-beratement didn't help one bit; in fact, it made everything worse. I saw myself as weak, so the relentless, painful cycle continued.

One time, after an exceptionally difficult day, I was standing in my kitchen and randomly stated to no one in particular, "I wish I had a gun." I didn't mean for anyone to hear me. Not my wife, who was also in the room, nor anyone else for that matter. This desperate statement was half wishful thinking and half insanity and, if the truth be known, I had no clue as to which end of the normalcy scale I belonged at that point. Can you imagine what must have gone through Robin's mind when I uttered that phrase? Or what if Jake had heard me? I'm sure I repeated that statement on many other occasions, so it wasn't just a one-time rambling.

At first, Robin just dismissed it, but after hearing me say it several times, she became very concerned for me, and rightly so. She eventually called my bereavement counselor and told him that she was terrified about what I might do.

Was I suicidal? In truth…no. I didn't have any plans on doing anything to harm myself. And besides, how could I do that to Robin and Jake? They needed me. However, I will share with you that I've often wondered what I would have done if there *had* been a firearm in the house. Then no planning would have been required. It's the million-dollar question…would I have pulled the trigger? I'll never know. But I can tell you this; there would have been a passionate debate within myself before I took that thought any further. I can only say that I am most grateful there are no guns in our house.

If you ever entertain those same kinds of thoughts, don't agonize about diagnosing yourself as crazy, because you're not. Believe me, depression can make you think and do things a "normal" person would never consider. As I mentioned in The Heavy Wet Blanket chapter, I was a "rookie" to depression. It wasn't something that ran in my family, so I wasn't fully prepared for this manner of thought. I'm telling you this because I now understand just how easy, and even inviting, it is to head down the wrong path. I can't drive it home strongly enough how much I wrestled with which route to take and how glad I am that I chose the one I eventually followed.

No one can begrudge you for thinking about taking the easy way out, but ask yourself this: What would your deceased child want you to do? Before you give these dark thoughts serious consideration, please read the chapter entitled "I Have a

Responsibility." I hope my words and insights will bring you back to the land of the living and convince you to do the right thing, though not necessarily the easy thing.

The bottom line is *you're* the one who's going to have to do the work if you are to push through this tragedy. Nobody else can do it for you. But never forget, there are many people who will be grateful to see you come out on the other side—and believe me, you will be one of them.

# GETTING THROUGH THE FIRST YEAR

## INITIAL COPING TACTICS

# IN SEARCH OF THERAPY

For the first month or so after Samantha died, I thought I could handle the flood of emotions that hit me, without the help of a therapist. *Therapy is a just bunch of hogwash, anyway,* I told myself. This was typical guy thinking, I suppose. In my opinion, men aren't usually open to going to therapists, and those who do are inclined not to tell their friends because they feel embarrassed.

I was no different. I thought: *How is talking about it going to fix the situation? It's not going to bring Samantha back. Besides, how is it going to make me feel better? I just have to work it out on my own, let time pass, and be strong. Tough it out.* I'll bet you've had these same thoughts...*I don't need to see some therapist. I can handle it on my own.*

However, in reality, my "go it alone" mindset wasn't working for me. More than my mental health was suffering. My *physical* health was seriously affected too; so much so, that my doctor demanded that I get my heart rate checked on a weekly basis.

The horrific feelings I was experiencing seemed almost inhumane. I questioned where they even came from, for I truly felt humans simply weren't "programmed" to experience, never mind deal with, this level of emotional trauma. It was enough to make the strongest of men go nuts!

Trying to process this amount of pain on your own, in my opinion, is futile. Where do you begin? How do you even sort out these unasked for feelings? How do you start the process of understanding them for what they are, discuss them, and then work them out? Having "been there, done that," I now believe it's impossible to do this on your own. It simply doesn't work.

The hard truth is, your world has been turned completely upside down. You're probably drowning in emotions that you never experienced before and can't explain, let alone handle. You've been hit in the heart with pain so incredibly deep and intense, you wonder how any human can endure it. Never, in your worst nightmares, did you imagine you would find yourself having to deal with the loss of your child. You can't even begin to conceive how to respond or what your next step should be. And if that weren't challenging enough, none of your friends has ever experienced the loss of a child either, so how in the world are they going to know how to help you?

In the face of all this, the question is not why you should seek help, but rather, why in the world *wouldn*'t you?

-   -   -

Shortly after Samantha's passing, Robin arranged for us to see a therapist together. After only two sessions, I found that going as a couple wasn't working for me because Robin dominated the conversation, making it difficult for me to get anything out of it. It wasn't Robin's fault; I just didn't know how it all worked and, being a typical guy, I was reluctant to fully open up and "spill the beans" to someone I didn't know.

For whatever reason, it seemed easier for Robin to communicate with this therapist than it did for me, perhaps because the therapist was a woman. I found myself struggling to say something and always seemed to hold back. During one session, the therapist said to me, "Jon, you're awfully quiet. What would *you* like to say?" To my surprise, as I listened to Robin and the therapist talk, I realized that Samantha's death had stirred up the feeling of anxiety, and I felt embarrassed to talk about this particular topic with her. I don't know why, but I didn't want the therapist to think I was a wimp. I realized I had nothing to prove to her. Down deep, I understood that my reservation to fully participate was illogical and unhelpful. Yet something more powerful was causing me to clam up.

Next, we tried the group therapy approach. About a month after Samantha died, we went to a meeting for a support group geared toward families who have experienced the loss of a parent, sibling, or child. I remember that night clearly, as if it just happened yesterday. It was a cold, rainy, dark night and we had a great deal of trouble even finding the building. I have to tell you, in all honesty, I didn't want to go. I didn't want to hear other people's sad stories and I certainly didn't want to talk about mine. I went because I wanted to be there for Jake and, quite frankly, because Robin forced me to go.

Any kids accompanying their parents went downstairs with a social worker while their parents stayed upstairs. We sat around a table in a group therapy session with a professional counselor, taking turns talking in detail about our personal situations.

One woman, who sat at the head of the table, struggled to withhold her tears the entire night. Finally, it was her turn to speak. Mind you, by now I had already listened to six horrible stories about family deaths, so I had pretty much reached my limit by the time she began to tell her story. She told us how her eldest son, who was about 12 years old at the time, had died after being hit by a car while riding his bike. Although the accident had happened about a year before, nonetheless, for this poor woman, it was as raw as if it had happened yesterday. She was still completely ripped apart by the death of her son.

At some point, her 11-year-old surviving son, who was two years younger than the brother who had passed, came upstairs to the "parent's room." I was immediately struck by how much this kid was hurting. Looking into his incredibly sad eyes, I could see how his grief betrayed his childhood, making him appear much older than his years. I couldn't stop looking at him and the sadness in his eyes.

While his mother kept talking about her situation, I didn't hear a word she said. I couldn't stop looking at her son. In no way, shape or form was he a normal 11-year-old child. He looked as if he had the weight of the world on his shoulders. I can't tell you how badly I felt for him and how depressed he made me feel. I was pulled into his grief, and it was like being punched in the stomach. I actually had trouble breathing.

As we were driving home, I had an epiphany. It felt like a stream of light coming down from the heavens, illuminating everything. Suddenly I could clearly see why this child had made me feel so upset. This poor kid had actually suffered a double tragedy, for not only had he lost his older brother, who happened to be his best friend, but he had also lost his mother in the aftermath! She had become so distraught from the accident that she could no longer function as a parent. Her continuing grief was doing terrible damage to herself and to her child.

I kept remembering my mother's words, "Don't let Jake lose that smile." I looked back at my Jake as he sat in his car seat and I thought about how innocent and angelic he seemed. Then I asked myself: – *Do I want my son to turn into that 11-year-old child I saw at the meeting? Do I want to become that woman? Could I risk being in that mental state for the rest of my life?*

It was at that moment that I realized three key things, and they were the three things that helped me get through the first year after Samantha's death.

First, I have a responsibility to Jake to continue to be his father to the best of my ability. I happen to be one of those guys who thinks a child needs *both* a mother and a father. Each brings a different perspective and has a different role in rearing a child.

I can't let Jake down. I can't turn into a depressed, drunk or drugged-out shell of a parent. I brought him into this world. He didn't ask to be here. I have to be a father to him.

Second, I have a responsibility to Robin, my wife. After all, she's hurting too, albeit in different ways. If I shut myself off to her and go into a never ending funk, how am I being a husband to her? I'm a man. A man *has* to provide, and I don't just mean money. A man has to be a true partner to his wife. Anything less and you're not a man.

And third, I have a responsibility to my business partners and employees. At that time, I was the sole sales person for my company. All those people were relying on me to be successful. How could I serve these people if I let myself turn into that woman I witnessed at the meeting?

This wonderful epiphany caused me to make a defining decision, one that put me on the road to recovery.

-   -   -

After that fateful night in the car, I concluded that this was something I couldn't handle on my own. I *did* need to speak with a professional.

Yet even after having my epiphany, I still waited about a month before I made an appointment. He was a therapist who helped people with general issues but didn't possess any expertise in dealing with extreme grief. Unfortunately, I neglected to ask him about his credentials in this area and just assumed he would know how to deal with grief. After a couple of sessions, however, I realized that my issues were way out of his league. He didn't seem to have a clue about what to ask me or, more importantly, what to say.

When he started off a session with, "What did you think about all the traffic out there today?" I knew I had the wrong person. I had just lost a child, for crying out loud! Did he really think I cared about the traffic?

I was hurting badly and couldn't waste any more time with this therapist, nor could I afford to have him learning on the job with me as his guinea pig. I needed help immediately. More than that, I needed a plan for healing and recovery, so that I would know there was a light at the end of the tunnel, however long that tunnel might be. I didn't care if it was going to take years, just as long as I had a plan. A plan would give me hope, and control. I hung onto that.

Finally in December 2006, three months after Samantha passed away, I found a bereavement counselor who had real experience with grief. Several of his clients were parents who had lost a child. Perfect! He had also counseled kids and teachers in the aftermath of an unexpected school death. As a matter of fact, after 9/11 he took a voluntary leave of absence from his job so he could travel to Ground Zero and provide counseling to survivors and their next of kin, as well as their rescuers.

In addition to all his valuable grief experience, we also made a personal connection. I found comfort in how much we were alike and how we shared common interests, like sports. He was a big fan of the Boston Red Sox and the New England Patriots. He was a runner and enjoyed working out. He also had a son. I felt completely at ease talking with him. He was *exactly* what I needed and was looking for.

Even with all this, the decision *still* wasn't easy. The thought of talking about my depression and how much I longed for Samantha was going to be the second most difficult thing I'd ever had to do (the first, needless to say, was watching her die and attending her funeral).

Think about it. There you are, exposing your fractured heart to this other person, this stranger, talking about some of the most painful and personal things you've ever experienced in your life. I couldn't help but obsess. *Was I ready for this challenge? Could I handle it? Wouldn't it just be easier to wallow in my sorrow; to shut the curtains, close the door, pull the covers over my head and never leave the comfort of my bed?*

As much as I knew I needed help, I also dreaded the pain that therapy would involve. Oh, I knew all about physical pain, because back in 2001 I had run a marathon. But this was different, wasn't it? This was going to be an emotional marathon, one that induced mental rather than physical pain. But then I challenged myself with the knowledge that running a marathon *is* half mental. Sure, you have to train to get yourself in shape, but at the end of the day, isn't it your mental toughness that gets you through the race?

Although therapy was different from anything I'd ever done before, I chose to look at it as a challenge. Not unlike running a marathon, it would take perseverance, mental toughness, and a total commitment. I decided if I was going to do it, I was going all in. I told myself, *What's the point if you're going to hold everything back? Don't leave anything on the field. If you want to get better, give it all you have. It's going to be incredibly painful, but worth it.*

I remembered what my Mom said – "Don't let your son lose his smile." And I reminded myself that I was *not* going to be like that woman at the group therapy session, whose son was so damaged. I was going to do it, and I was going to succeed. And with that attitude, I began my therapy.

-   -   -

I was so nervous about taking this journey, and had worked myself into such a state, that by the time I arrived for my first session, I thought I was going to faint. My heart was beating so hard, I actually held my hand to my chest because I felt that if I didn't, my heart would literally jump out of it!

Initially, I saw my bereavement counselor for one hour, once a week. These sessions were so important to me that, even though I was the only sales person at my company at the time, I would decline meetings with potential clients if it conflicted with my therapy. The sessions became my top priority.

Doing "the grief work," as he called it, was the goal of every session. Either I'd choose the topic I wanted to cover, or he'd ask me questions about how I was doing and we'd take it from there. We didn't always talk about my grief, either. Sometimes we'd discuss my work issues or the residual anxiety I began feeling after Samantha's passing. This was one of the advantages of going to a grief therapist, because I was able to discuss everyday issues, as well as the difficult ones surrounding Samantha's death. I got the best of both rolled into one person.

After about eight months or so of weekly sessions, I started to feel better, and so I began going every other week. And, as even more time passed, it became every three weeks, until finally, after about three years of hard work, it became once a month, which is the schedule I'm on now.

Throughout the course of this book, I'll be recounting many of the conversations my therapist and I have had, and continue to have. One the main reasons for sharing such intimate dialogues is to show how a trained bereavement counselor might approach guys like you and me. By letting you "listen in," I hope you'll see how this process can be of tremendous value to you, too. Although therapy is a personal decision, and you may respond to your grief very differently, I think there are many lessons in my experience that you may find useful.

First, don't be afraid to ask for help. I can't stress this enough: Know when to say *when*. If you're like me, in the beginning you're going to be stubborn and try to figure things out on your own. Don't be a martyr. You're not suffering from an ankle injury that will eventually heal itself. We're talking about extreme mental anguish that can and will impact every aspect of your life, if you don't deal with it properly. If you reach the point where you just can't manage anymore, give yourself permission to reach out and get help.

Second, look for a therapist or a group that really understands the deep grief you are experiencing. Not all therapists are trained in this field, so if you decide to go down the path of personal therapy, ask the therapist about his or her credentials in this specific area. Insist on finding a bereavement counselor, not just a general therapist. And don't be afraid to "try them out" until you find a counselor you can connect with. Opening up about your pain and anguish is hard enough; you need someone you trust and feel good about if you are to do it successfully.

You may also find help from a support group. Although the first group I tried was not for me, I did find a group later on that I am still involved with. Here in Massachusetts, there's a group specifically for fathers who have lost a child called "Father's Forever." There's also a group called "Compassionate Friends." You may find similar groups where you live. If not, perhaps you'll pick up the gauntlet and start one yourself.

Finally, I urge you to remember that you can't afford to let your grief completely overcome you to the point that you are unable to function. If you feel that you're heading in that direction, think about the people who are counting on you. What would happen to them if you went off the deep end? If you have a surviving child, put yourself in that child's shoes. How would you feel if you not only lost your sibling, but also "lost" your father to depression? Don't you think that would be a double blow? Doesn't your surviving child deserve better?

There's no right or wrong way when it comes to seeking help. Everyone has their own preferences and needs. To this day, my therapist and I keep the plan pretty flexible. When events such as Samantha's birthday or funeral anniversary are approaching, I might need to see him once a week until that event passes and I'm feeling steady once again. The point is, don't say to yourself, "I'm only going for eight sessions and that's it," or, "I'll give therapy one shot and if it doesn't work, I'm out." Keep an open mind. Give it a chance, and let the process work itself out.

Trust your gut. You'll know when it's working for you, and you'll know when you have made progress and can scale back the therapy. When you reach the point where you say to your bereavement counselor at the beginning of the session, "I really don't have anything to talk about today," *that's* when you'll know that you've successfully made it through the worst of the bereavement process.

If you seek the help you need, I know that day will come for you, too.

# FANTASY ISLAND

I used to fantasize about Samantha all the time. Whenever I played with Jake, I envisioned Samantha being present and playing along with us. I could feel her on my lap, hear her laughing, and I convinced myself that she and Jake were interacting and having fun playing together, just like always. I think I may have even said to Jake once or twice, "Make sure you share with Samantha."

One particular fantasy episode stands out in my memory. Right after Samantha died, I took Jake to his swimming lesson as usual. As I sat there watching him, my mind began to wander. Inevitably, I began thinking about Samantha, and soon I *believed* that she was sitting on my lap. I began talking to her, hugging, kissing and tickling her, as if she were *right there* with me, in person. I even started saying and doing funny things with my face to make her laugh. Man, did that feel good! I'm quite sure that if anyone actually saw me, they would have concluded that I had lost my mind.

Fantasizing about Samantha's presence became a habit. Even when Jake and I were playing with his miniature cars or with toy tools in our basement, I always *saw* Samantha right there with us. I'd *watch* while she and Jake talked and laughed, just a normal brother and his baby sister playing together.

This fantasizing provided me with what few happy moments I was able to experience during my early grieving period. In that sense, bringing her back in my imagination was a good thing.

When I brought up my fantasizing episodes to the bereavement counselor, he asked, "Why do you do this?"

"Because it makes me feel good," I answered.

"How long do you plan on doing this?"

"Forever because I always want to feel Samantha with me."

"When you do this fantasizing, are you able to concentrate completely on Jake?"

"No," I admitted.

"Don't you think Jake, even though he's only three and a half and doesn't have an adult's vocabulary, is hurting too?"

"Of course he is," I said. "Samantha was his best friend. They loved each other very much. I know I'm biased, but they seemed to be more connected than most siblings their age."

"Doesn't Jake need you now more than ever?"

"Yes."

"What about his mental health? Don't you want him to deal with his loss while retaining his sense of humor and overall happiness?"

"Of course I do," I said. "Why are you asking me these questions?"

"Because when you fantasize, you're not there for Jake and he can pick up on that. He needs you! For him to get through this and come out the other side as a normal functioning human being who adds value to society, he needs you! He needs your support and love. Samantha's dead. There's nothing you can do about that now. No matter how much you fantasize about her, she's not coming back. Jake is here. He is your priority now."

My bereavement counselor went on, "Jon, you can't be in two places at once. If you're fantasizing, then you're not really engaging with Jake. You're not there to pick up on any of his subtle clues that indicate whether he's sad or just wants a big hug from his daddy. He was already feeling horrible about the loss of his baby sister. Why make him feel that he's been abandoned by you, as well?"

That was a point I hadn't considered. I had already vowed I would not abandon Jake by wallowing in my own grief. But I had not realized that my fantasies, while giving me peace and comfort, could be short-changing Jake. While I was with Jake physically during these times, I was not totally with him mentally and emotionally. My mind was elsewhere, locked into a happier place that provided me with the comfort that was missing in my real life without Samantha.

My counselor also said my fantasizing was interfering with my own ability to work through the grieving process, which he described as an evolutionary journey from one level to the next. The early phases of grief, while mentally difficult, are physically challenging as well. Then, as you continue to conquer each phase, the later levels become easier to overcome. But if you get stuck on one level, you can become stagnant and immobilized for too long, and your recovery stops progressing. You need to keep moving if you want to complete the journey.

Perhaps this analogy, while not perfect, will help you to relate a little better. I once saw a television show about how the Navy trains its elite SEALs teams. During training, the recruits are given very difficult tasks to complete and once they successfully do so, they're able to move on to the next level. If they make it past the first three weeks and then the dreaded "Hell Week," the challenges become more "reasonable," like running six miles on the beach or target practice; still pretty demanding tasks, but not nearly as overwhelming. The point is, these latter evolutions aren't as mentally and physically challenging as the ones in the first four weeks of the program.

I think the grieving process is very similar. You must work through one stage at a time, and there are no shortcuts. As my bereavement counselor told me, "If you want to get from point A to point B and there's a body of water separating the two points, you need to cross the bridge. If you don't cross the bridge, you'll be stuck in point A forever."

Getting "stuck" in the grieving process can become problematic and stall your efforts to successfully push through it all. By fantasizing that Samantha was still interacting with me, I got myself "stuck." I wasn't accepting her death or facing it head on, nor was I dealing with the raw, terrible emotions it had caused within me. While this fantasy world kept me in a "feel good place," ultimately it sabotaged my progress. If my intention was to get mentally healthier, I had to stop fantasizing that Samantha was still with me, and start dealing with the reality that she was gone.

Oh, I knew my counselor was right, but I still didn't want to stop. It felt too good. And, in all honesty I feared that once I stopped fantasizing about Samantha, I might eventually forget about her, a possibility I couldn't bear to think about. I never wanted to forget her or what it was like having her in my life.

This debate raged within me for a good month or so. In the end, I finally had to accept his point and stop the fantasizing. If I ever expected to find my way back from this horrific loss, I simply had to remove myself, of my own volition, from that world of make-believe. I would have to give Samantha up again.

"Short term pain for long term gain" became my motto for survival.

-   -   -

Making the decision was only half the battle. Actually carrying it out was yet another thing all together. It was clearly a "mind over matter" exercise. Whenever I began to fantasize about Samantha or picture her playing with Jake, I would say aloud, "STOP!". Again, people who heard me, and I'm sure they did, must have thought I was crazy. For the first few weeks,

I must have yelled out "STOP" every two minutes.

I have to say that this decision was one of the most poignant moments in my entire bereavement journey. I was giving up my "security blanket" and venturing into terrifying places. Fantasizing that Samantha was still with me was one of the few things that had given me any joy, and here I was about to give that up. I couldn't help feeling conflicted. On the one hand, I might be exacerbating my sense of loss by ceasing my fantasy visits with Samantha. On the other hand, stopping these fantasies would perhaps free me up to concentrate on doing the tough grief work.

It should have been a simple decision, and yet I debated the heck out of it. Ultimately, I trusted my bereavement counselor, that he knew what he was talking about, and that he had only my best interests in mind when he told me what I needed to do.

"Fantasy Island" was a pretty accurate term for where I was at in those days. When I engaged in one of my fantasy episodes, I completely isolated myself from the rest of the world and all the people in it. In hindsight, I now recognize that in addition to stalling my progress, fantasizing kept other people at arm's length, people who were genuinely concerned about me and yet felt uneasy talking with me whenever I ventured into my Fantasy Island mode. I was told that I would get this far away look on my face, a look that proclaimed, "Do not disturb." So, can you blame them?

One final thought on this topic--for those of you who regularly visit your child's grave site, if it makes you feel good, then by all means, keep doing it. But, if it's preventing you from letting go and moving through the bereavement process, then you really need to stop, at least until you're ready to take yourself to the next evolutionary step in your healing. Once there, then I suggest you resume your visits on a regular basis.

The message here is, be careful that you don't get trapped in habits or rituals that might make you feel better, but keep you stuck in your grief and separated from those you care about, and depend on you. Fantasy Island is both a fantasy and an island. Don't allow yourself to get lost there.

# DRUGS TO THE RESCUE

I remember the exact date when I decided to take the plunge and try anti-depressant medication. It was December 19, 2006, a little over three months after Samantha's death. Believe me, it wasn't an easy decision.

First of all, I hate taking pills. Second, and more importantly, I believed that I was *supposed* to feel unspeakable pain, for that's the natural consequence of losing a child. Besides, wouldn't I be "cheating" if I eased that pain with an anti-depressant?

My bereavement counselor and I endlessly debated that topic for the first month of my therapy. However, while this conversation was going on, my health began to deteriorate. My blood pressure and heart rate were at dangerously high levels. I couldn't sleep. I was a nervous wreck. My stomach was constantly churning. I felt on the verge of suffering a heart attack, or developing a bleeding ulcer--or both.

My bereavement counselor would say to me, "Jon, do you think Samantha would want you to be in this much pain?" To which I would respond, "No, but I *need* to feel this pain. How else am I going to grieve for her? I'm supposed to be in this pain. If I'm not, then I'm not going through the grieving process correctly." Right or wrong, that's how I saw it.

Logically, I knew that the counselor made sense. Of course Samantha wouldn't want me to ache the way I did. But I just couldn't bring myself to ease the pain with anti-depressants, either. Like most guys, I wanted to "tough it out." Taking pills, in my mind, was being a wimp and guys are supposed to be strong. I thought, *I'm a man. I can handle this. I'm not going to take the easy way out.*

While this debate raged between my counselor and me, I went to see my primary physician for my annual physical. My heart rate and blood pressure were off the charts. He was so alarmed that he immediately hooked me up to an EKG machine to monitor my heart rate. I'd never had that test before in my life, as I'm a pretty healthy guy. Plus, I'd never had heart problems and there wasn't a history of heart disease in my immediate family. He recommended that I check in with him on a weekly basis so he could look at and listen to my heart. My wife started to worry about my health, and so did I.

It got to the point where the stress was just too much for me to handle. It was, quite literally, wearing my body down. Not only that, but I was crying a lot, too. Riding home after work seemed to be the worst time of the day for me. Several times a week, trying to drive home, I'd be balling my eyes out, to the point of having to pull over to the side of the road to avoid having an accident.

The handwriting was on the wall, and so on that December day in 2006, I told my therapist that I was ready to consider taking anti-depressants. We talked about the plusses and minuses, the potential side effects, and the potential benefits. He advised me that taking this medication wouldn't take the emotional pain away, but would provide a floor of sorts, below which my depression would not be able to fall.

This was appealing to me. I thought, *Wouldn't it be good, both physically and emotionally, to "take the edge off a bit"? Wouldn't it feel much better to have a day in which I didn't feel like I was going to have a heart attack, an ulcer or an anxiety attack? Wouldn't it be good to be able to really talk about Samantha, her life, what she meant to me, her death and how that affected me without having a panic attack or breaking down crying?*

The answer was "yes" to all of those questions. Besides,

if taking this step would make me better able to work through the grieving process, then that was enough for me. I decided to take the anti-depressants, and let me tell you, it was one of the hardest yet best decisions I made during those early days of my grieving process.

- - -

The medication started taking effect right away. Within the first week, I began feeling better. I still felt tremendous hurt, but I didn't cry hysterically while driving home from work anymore. Even the pain in my stomach, which felt like someone was constantly drilling a hole right through my gut, started to ease up a bit.

Other changes happened over time. One striking difference was that I could finally look at babies, especially baby girls, again. I still couldn't hold them, but I was no longer compelled to avoid them. This was a huge gain for me. Only three months earlier, I couldn't even be in the same room with a baby girl, let alone look at her.

The medication significantly improved my therapy. With my anxiety eased and my depression no longer spinning out of control, I was able to dive deeply into the therapy sessions on a regular basis—to a degree I never could have handled otherwise.

There were some downsides to the medication. The biggest was "air headedness." My short term memory and reading recall took a nose dive, and I often found it hard to focus. As these side effects began to intensify, and as the years went by and the gut-wrenching pain began to subside, I started noticing these side effects more and more. I found myself having to write everything down, or else I'd forget. I would start a newspaper article on the front page, flip to an inside page to continue the story, and I'd forget what the article was about. I'd have to re-read it from the beginning.

In the summer of 2009, about two and a half years after I started taking the anti-depressants, I felt well enough to consider making a new decision: coming off them. This sparked the same debate that I had waged when I started, only in reverse. Now I had to evaluate the pros and cons of coming *off* the medication. The biggest question I posed to my counselor was, "Am I going to get hit with another one of those Heavy Wet Blanket episodes again?" This really concerned me, because I just couldn't stomach the thought of going through *that* again.

The timing I had chosen-- the third anniversary of Samantha's death and funeral was just around the corner—also made it difficult. I couldn't help but wonder, *Was now the best time for me to stop taking these meds?* Tough decision.

Plus, ever since Samantha passed away, I've hated the fall season. The change in weather, the anniversary; they all bring back horrible memories and leave me feeling down.

My wife, Robin, was also concerned about the timing. "Why don't you just wait until after September?" she urged me. "You know we go to the cemetery every September, so why don't you wait until that's over before you start going off the meds?"

Other people said to me, "You'd never go on a diet just before Thanksgiving, because you wouldn't be able to keep your commitment." Thinking back on it, this analogy makes a lot of sense. Why try to come off anti-depressant medication right before the anniversary of your child's death?

My bereavement counselor and I discussed all the potential negatives, but what kept coming back to me was the fact that I had made such great strides. I felt strong again. I had been through the first, second and almost third year since Samantha died. If I could get through that, I thought, I'm finally okay to come off the meds. Besides, the only way I could truly know whether my mental strength had improved sufficiently to stop taking my meds was to stop taking them, right? So in mid-July of 2009, almost three years after Samantha died, I decided to come off the medication.

Having been on the anti-depressants for so long, I understandably had a lot of trepidation about the change. Yet at the same time, I felt a bit excited. Coming off the meds would be proof positive that my life was somewhat "normal" once again. My physician put together a tapering off program that would have me completely medication-free in six weeks.

The weaning process was not as bad as I expected, though it wasn't easy. I experienced a mixture of anxiety, headaches, irritability and manic feelings. I had real trouble relaxing. On the plus side, I had more energy and more focus, and my libido skyrocketed.

And I knew, if the depression came back, I could always resume the meds again.

- - -

It turned out I was not as ready as I thought I was. As the anniversary got closer, and the medication was completely out of my system, I began to feel overwhelmed. The anxiety and depression hit me hard. I remember one day quite vividly. It was a Wednesday, less than a week before the anniversary, and I was at work. I was a basket case, and I couldn't stop crying. I didn't think I could make it through the day, let alone the days before and after the anniversary. Plus, the tornado in my stomach, which I hadn't felt in a year, was back with a vengeance. After all the bereavement work I had done, I hadn't expected to go this low emotionally. But the whole experience was a jolt to my system, and it was simply too much to handle.

I called my doctor and started back up on the medication.

I chose to view this decision as a win rather than a setback. I didn't say to myself, *You weakling. You failed. You're back on the meds.* Rather, I congratulated myself for recognizing how helpful medication was and for taking a necessary action.

I think there are two lessons here. One is recognizing the importance and value of anti-depressants, when taken under the direction of a therapist or physician. These medications exist to make you feel better. There's nothing inherently wrong with taking meds if you need them, and they are not a sign of weakness. In my case, they helped me to function during the worst ordeal any parent can imagine. Most importantly, because they lifted me up emotionally, they empowered me to hit the grief work head on. In fact, I believe the anti-depressants made it possible for me to do my most difficult and important work in therapy.

The other lesson is to accept that you have your own level of coping ability. It's not your fault if you need to take meds, nor is it your fault if you can't give them up when you think you should. In fact, there is no "should." Your decisions about medication are exactly that: *your* decisions.

Of course, it goes without saying that medication taken on your own, without a doctor's supervision, is a dangerous and destructive course. I've addressed this temptation in other chapters. Like hitting the bottle, escaping with the help of meds may be appealing, but there is no progress or healing in that direction.

That said, taking medication with the supervision of your therapist can be a wise and empowering decision. So don't feel bad if you need meds to help you cope, or if you find you can't give them up yet. No one will begrudge your decisions about this. You must do *whatever* it takes, and if that includes meds, don't feel you need to explain or apologize to anyone. You are the one suffering extreme grief. You are the one who must find the path forward.

# THE SHOCK IS OVER

## REALITY KICKS IN

# THE NEW REALITY

Once the initial shock had passed and the realization hit that my baby had died, I began to feel different, physiologically as well as psychologically. Everything had changed--from the way I thought, to the way I felt, especially my stress level. More than that, my entire outlook on life shifted in a way I never believed was possible. At first, I didn't like this new sense of being. It disturbed me because it wasn't me, or at least "the me" I knew.

The realization that things were forever altered hit me one day as I stood in the checkout line at a neighborhood store. The simple act of going shopping, until that day a normal task, suddenly felt totally foreign to me. Somehow I'd become disconnected from all the other people in line. From where I stood, the others didn't seem to have a care in the world. They were just casually picking up a few items to take home to their families. And while I was doing the same, I was anything *but* carefree. There was a battle going on within me, between the forces of depression and anxiety on one side, and my struggle to stay focused and remain in the present on the other. My mind was a million miles away.

I began to obsess over this change. *Is this the way it's going to be from now on? Is this the new Jon? Will the old Jon ever reappear? Am I always going to feel different from those who'll never truly know what I've been through and continue to go through? Will I ever feel "normal" again? For that matter, what does "normal" feel like?; it's been so long since I felt that way...*

As I write this, it has been close to three years since Samantha left us, and now I have a hard time remembering that I ever had a different life. The fact is, I'm now the father of a child who passed away. That's my new identity and I'm stuck with it for the rest of my days.

Losing a child changes you in ways you can't begin to fathom. The change has an almost physical existence. I feel it in my gut, my core, my bones, in the air that I breathe. It's this "thing" that's always out there…and it never goes away. Sure, I can be distracted for short periods of time, but it always comes back. This "thing" waits in the wings--confident in the knowledge that it has me in its grip.

- - -

Recently, after a round of golf with a couple of my friends and a newcomer to our league, we all decided to grab some dinner and a few beers at the clubhouse. As we sat around the table enjoying the beautiful summer night, the newcomer started talking about one of his neighbors, a guy who had recently lost his nineteen-year-old son in a car accident. The guy clearly felt awful for his friend and said, "How can he deal with this? I can't even imagine what it's like. I could never handle it." I sat in silence, not knowing what to say. I wanted to raise my hand and say, "I know what it's like. I lost my daughter almost three years ago," but I was uncomfortable, so I simply kept sipping my beer and hoped the other two guys would change the subject. It's moments like these that take you into the realm of separateness from the rest of the world. It is a horrible, lonely place.

I tried describing this place to one of my business partners. I said, with more than a little jealousy, "You get to go home and be with your kids and enjoy a normal, happy life. I don't. On top of all the normal stresses in life, like stretching your paycheck to cover the monthly bills and still have enough left over to enjoy life with your family, I have all this other stuff going on in my head. I never have peace…ever! Most men can go home after work and that's it for them--time to relax and enjoy the evening with their family. Not for me. I'd give anything to be able to just go home and relax...period!"

Of course no one really knows what goes on in someone else's life. We just naturally assume "the grass is greener on the other side." But that's my point. I couldn't see anything BUT the perfection of everyone else's life and the unjust imperfection of mine. That's what this grief was doing to me. It was distorting everything around me.

In the beginning, even going home after work was difficult because peace no longer existed there. Home become a place of pain for me. No longer would my baby come running down the hallway to greet me with arms raised, yelling "Dada" and waiting to be scooped up in my arms and smothered with hugs and kisses. That's what it should be like when you get home from work. That's what life is all about. But not anymore.

Once I got home, the day would deteriorate from bad to worse. At least at work, I was busy and had distractions to keep my mind occupied. I actually enjoyed going back to work, solely for that reason. At least it got me out of the house and kept me from dwelling on my situation. Coming home became like a sucker punch in the face or a kick in the groin, and only reinforced the void. At home, I simply couldn't escape from the loss of Samantha.

Relaxing in front of the TV and enjoying an evening with my family, like most "normal" people do, wasn't an option. My mind was never at ease. It kept re-playing the exact same scene over and over again: the end of Samantha's life. And with those thoughts came the unbearable pain and the unrelenting fear that an anxiety attack was about to strike.

If you have lost a child, no matter what you do or how

hard you try to fit in, you are apart from the rest of your friends in a deep and profound way. There's no way around this fact. You *are* the guy who's lost a child. You *are* different now. There's no question about changing it. All you can do is accept it. It's the new reality and you will simply have to learn how to deal with it for the rest of your life.

The real question is this: Will you allow this new reality to change you in a negative way, or in a positive way?

- - -

People sometimes ask me, "Are you angry?" The answer I give now is, "No, not anymore." What does being bitter or angry get you anyway? What does it accomplish? Not only will it cause health problems--trust me, I know--but ultimately it ends up driving away the people who love you and want to support you the most. No one wants to be around an angry, bitter person. Nobody!

It's easy to be angry at the world and it's perfectly natural to be so. You may even be justified in your anger. But what would your lost child want? What do your surviving loved ones want? I know this for certain: they would not want you to live the rest of your life in bitterness.

I've seen people who have gone through this kind of loss and remained bitter and "mad at the world." You know those people; you've seen them. They don't smile, they don't engage in conversation, and their facial expression is riddled with pain and misery. Their eyes have a distant, removed, or even a sort of dead look to them.

My grandmother on my mother's side lost a 32-year-old daughter to cancer. This happened before I was born, so I never knew my grandmother before that loss, but I can tell you this: I hardly ever saw her smile. The death of her daughter had completely destroyed her, turning her into a miserable person. She ended up a bitter, angry woman with very few friends. Nobody could put up with her. She lived another forty-years or so that way.

If you've suffered the heartbreak of losing a child, you will feel anger. You will feel apart from the world. Those reactions are unavoidable. But you don't have to embrace those feelings as a way of living. In fact, you must not embrace them, for the road never gets any easier that way, but it WILL get lonelier.

My advice is not to focus on the doom and gloom. Force yourself to turn away from this manner of thinking. You're here on this Earth for a finite time, so how do you want to spend it? Do you want to feel miserable? Do you want life to pass you by as you observe it through a negative lens? Or, do you want to live the rest of your days making new memories, potentially happy ones, and being an active participant?

Things *are* going to be different, and nothing will *ever* be the same, but you do have control over how you choose to respond and live out the rest of your life. Your New Reality can go either way. I say make the choice your lost child would want you to make. Choose happiness.

# ANGRY WITH GOD

I said in the last chapter that I was no longer angry. That is not quite true.

Since Samantha's death, I haven't been to our synagogue a single time, because frankly, in the context of religion, I'm pissed off. Why was my baby taken from me? What did Samantha do to deserve this? What did *I* do to deserve this? With all the sick people in the world who abuse kids and do terrible things to other human beings, why me? And tell me this--why are *they* still here, when my baby isn't?

Before all this, I was a Reform Jew, meaning that I observed the High Holy Days and all the other major religious holidays of our faith. But I did it out of tradition, not necessarily belief, despite having observant parents who tried to instill the faith within me. Religion was not part of my everyday life. For me, faith was not going to be a source of strength for coping with my loss.

If you do have faith yourself, please don't take this chapter personally. I respect whatever anyone wants to believe. I understand that many people, perhaps most, find comfort in their faith. I know this is true of my friends. If you have that kind of belief yourself, then you don't need this chapter, and probably shouldn't even read it. You already have something to anchor you, to give you answers, and you have a community that brings comfort to you. In many ways, I am envious of people who have that. But for me, turning to God in this matter is not really an option. I just can't choose to believe in an idea that makes no sense to me.

This chapter is for fathers who, like me, do not find the answers they need in religion, and probably feel angry about it all. It would be nice to believe that it's all been planned out, and everything happens for a reason. But what if you just can't accept that? Maybe my thoughts can help. At least, you'll know that you are not the only father who feels that way.

-   -   -

My friends, who are of different denominations, and who rely on their faith to one degree or another to get them through difficult times, tried to comfort me by saying, "Samantha's in a better place right now. She's with God."

Of course, I knew they were only trying to help, and in fact were telling me what they would tell themselves, if they were in the same situation. But their words did not comfort me at all. They made me angry.

I wanted to say, "Are you crazy? How could a baby be in a better place by being dead? A baby belongs here, not in heaven or wherever else we're supposed to go when we die. My baby belongs right here, in my arms, playing with her brother Jake, singing and dancing in her room, or snuggling and having a book read to her. That's where she belongs…no ifs, ands or buts!"

Others would tell me, "There are no answers. It's God's plan." This made no sense to me either. What kind of plan has God taking an innocent little girl? And why would I want to praise that God and give Him thanks?

I can understand a merciful and benevolent God taking a sick child, one who is condemned to lead a life that none of us would want them to endure, and by doing so ease the pain of that child and of his or her family. In a situation like that, I can comprehend the statement, "This child is now in a better place." But my Samantha was a pretty healthy baby. There was no mercy in ending her life.

- - -

It's customary in the Jewish faith to have a ceremony, called the "unveiling," one year after the funeral, where a headstone is placed on the grave.  As the day for the gathering approached, I started feeling anxious, for it would be my first visit since the funeral to the place that now held my daughter.  I was so nervous, in fact, that about a week before the event, I went to the cemetery in an effort to prepare myself.  On the way, I stopped at the local pool club.  After a bit, as I was getting ready to leave for the cemetery, the family sitting next to me said, "Why are you leaving so early?  Where are you going?"

"To a place I hope you never have to go," I said.

They looked bewildered, and one said, "What are you talking about?"

So I told them, "I'm headed to the cemetery to visit Samantha."

They looked at me with sheer horror.  I could see what they were thinking.  *I can't even begin to imagine what that's like.  I don't know what I'd do if I had to face that reality.*  Talk about a conversation killer.  Here they were, relaxing and about to head home for dinner with their kids, and I was off to the cemetery to visit one of mine.  This was a clear example of how estranged my life had become from the rest of the world, and I knew it wasn't going to change.

Needless to say, I had many sessions with my bereavement counselor leading up to the event, and I had talked with other people who had been to unveilings as well, so I had a pretty good idea of what to expect.  I figured whatever it took, I would do it.  But I wasn't prepared.  How could I be?

The whole experience was surreal.  I kept thinking to myself, *What the heck am I doing here?  My child isn't dead.*

*This is just a bad dream I'm having.* I felt as if I had been scooped up and placed on some distant, alien planet. Nothing around me was right. Perhaps a better description would be to call it an "out of body experience," only in reverse. It was my physical self that had wandered off to the wrong world, leaving my real self behind. It couldn't be me who was actually there. Never in a million years did I imagine that my child would die and that I'd be spending a beautiful Sunday afternoon visiting her grave. It was incomprehensible. My brain couldn't process something as horrible as that.

As I was sitting at the grave, I started thinking about a conversation from several years before, a conversation that now seemed eerily prescient. A woman I used to work with had lost her 20-year-old son in a car accident. Several months later, I met her for breakfast and shared with her that Robin and I were planning on starting a family. I wanted her advice because, as I explained to her, "I'd love to have kids, but I'm scared. What if one of my kids dies before I do? I couldn't handle it. That's why I'm afraid to have kids."

She said, "I'm grateful for the time I had with my son. If I were young enough to have more kids, I would make the decision again in a heartbeat."

Now several years later, here I was at the cemetery, the parent of a child who had passed away. The thing that I feared the most had come to pass. I just couldn't believe it!

I kept thinking, *Okay, I'm here. Now what am I supposed to do? Am I supposed to talk to the grave, cry, or what?* Instead, I just sat there and stared at the spot where the gravestone was going to go. My heart was pounding out of my chest. I was sweating profusely and felt extremely lightheaded. I was afraid I might have an anxiety attack. *Breathe deeply,* I told myself. *Just keep breathing deeply.* This calmed me down to the point where I could finally "talk" to Samantha. I spent an hour or so there, filling her in on what had been going on with the family since she had passed. I told her how much we loved her and missed her, and I asked her if our lives would ever be the same.

Only silence answered me.

The unveiling itself was a short ceremony attended by about 15 family members and officiated by our rabbi. I was numb throughout the entire thing, so I didn't really hear anything that was said. I was there physically, and that was about it. Simply put, it was like reliving the funeral all over again.

I couldn't help thinking that the whole event was merely adding insult to injury. First God had taken my child, and now He was making me relive the funeral. After that, I decided I wanted nothing more to do with God or religion. For me, personally, they simply did not provide any answers, only more pain and anger.

Each year, on Yom Kippur, the holiest day in the Jewish religion, it is said that some names are inscribed in the Book of Life, and some are inscribed in the Book of Death. And each year I ask, "Who inscribed Samantha's name in the Book of Death, and why?"

# MY HOME IS STILL MY CASTLE

I remember distinctly the first time I came home from work, following Samantha's death. Usually, she would be the first to greet me at the door. She'd be in the family room playing with Jake and would spot me coming in from the garage. In a flash, she'd come running down the hallway with her arms up waiting to be picked up, shouting "Dada!" I'd scoop her into my arms, give her a huge hug and a kiss and then, in return, I'd receive a loving pat on the back while she planted a big, wet kiss on my cheek. Those were some of the best kisses I ever got and I never wiped them off.

Next, I'd get attacked by Jake. He'd tear down the hallway yelling "Daddy!", jump into my arms and give me a big hug. Then I'd carry the two of them into the kitchen where I'd greet my wife, Robin. This was how I ended my work day, every day. And like most people, the stresses and problems from a day at work would vanish as soon as I saw and heard the kids bee-lining it down the hallway. It doesn't get any better than that.

But now it had all changed. When I opened the door from the garage into the house coming home that day, the only thing that greeted me was silence, overwhelming and surreal. My whole body began to shake and I felt as if I was going to either pass out or throw up. No Samantha... no "Dada!" No big hug, pat on the back, or wet kiss.

There are no words to describe how I felt. The English language just doesn't provide the vocabulary to express something of this magnitude. Maybe it could be likened to how astronaut Neal Armstrong struggled to describe his feelings when his foot first hit the surface of the moon. How do you describe emotions that big?

The next day was no different, nor the day after that.

Week after week, I came home from work, and my daughter was no longer there to greet me. The reality of her absence made it brutally clear that this wasn't a dream. She was really dead and she wasn't coming back.

At the risk of sounding cliché, the entire house had this immense dark cloud hanging over it and Samantha's absence permeated every space. Being home in the period shortly after she died made me feel as if I was walking in quicksand, where every move, every word, every action took a supreme effort on my part.

Even our dog, Maggie, was hurting. Maggie's a pretty dog with blonde fur and contrasting dark brown paws, making her look as if she's wearing socks. Maggie and Samantha were best friends and clearly loved one another. Samantha couldn't pronounce the word "Maggie," so she called her "Mammie." In fact, "Mammie" was one of the first words Samantha ever spoke.

Because Samantha was a lot smaller than Jake, I think Maggie felt a protective responsibility to be her "body guard." Maggie has always been a peaceful, friendly, loving dog, yet whenever a stranger, even a grandmotherly type, got too close to Samantha's stroller, Maggie would growl, putting that person on notice. Like most toddlers, Samantha didn't know how to pat the dog correctly and would often end up hitting Maggie instead. But Maggie didn't seem to mind at all. I think she knew that Samantha was just a little child and took it stoically.

A few days after Samantha died a woman rang our doorbell with our Maggie in tow. She had found her smack dab in the middle of the road in front of our house, just standing there looking up and down and all around. Because this was a pretty busy street, we had one of those invisible electric dog fences placed around the yard. We were vigilant in making sure that

Maggie never left our yard unattended, so you can only imagine our disbelief as to how this could have happened. Why had Maggie left the yard? What was she thinking? She must have had a purpose in mind. Robin and I talked about it, and it is our belief that Maggie was looking for *her* Samantha. I'm very grateful to that woman for protecting Maggie. I don't know what I would have done had a car injured her...or worse. She's part of our family.

Maggie continued to mope around the house, just like the rest of us. Then she developed a weird habit of licking her paws, almost non-stop. She licked so obsessively that her paws eventually became discolored. Maggie would also hang out in Samantha's bedroom, something she does to this day. Robin thinks she can "see" or sense Samantha's presence and it gives her comfort. There were many times when I couldn't find Maggie. I'd call for her, try to bribe her with some cheese, yet she wouldn't come. Eventually, I learned to look in Samantha's room and sure enough, there she'd be, just lying on the floor next to Samantha's crib.

- - -

About a year ago, we had some new furniture delivered to the house. Our neighbor thought it was a moving truck, so the next day she asked, "Are you guys moving?" The very idea of moving struck me as odd. Robin and I never discussed or even considered moving out of our home. This house gave us comfort, and it held wonderful memories of Samantha. Why rip ourselves up and move to a new, antiseptic house? Plus, adding a move to the turmoil we were already experiencing would have put us all in emotional overload.

Over time, I adjusted to the void of not having a "welcome home" greeting from Samantha. It became a fact of life, my new life, from now on. While I continually fought the feelings of depression, often brought on by returning home, still I didn't want our house to be just a place of doom and gloom.

Perhaps the biggest reason we didn't choose to move was because Robin and I didn't want to run away. For better or worse, this was our home. And a home is more than shelter. A home provides fond memories, and when bad things happen, it provides the safe haven that is needed to grieve. In our opinion, it's all part and parcel of life. So we decided to stay in our home...Samantha's home, Jake's home, and our dog Maggie's home.

# COPING IN SOCIAL
# SITUATIONS

# THEY JUST DON'T KNOW WHAT TO SAY

We all know how different men and women are when it comes to dealing with emotional subjects. I think the difference is both in our DNA, and in how we're raised. From the time we're little boys, we're treated differently than our sisters, no matter the age. It was always okay for a little girl to cry on the playground or hug her mommy and daddy in front of her friends, but not us boys. And whenever we did show our emotions, we'd end up having to deal with some pretty unpleasant ramifications. The rule on the playground for boys, even very young ones, was that crying wasn't cool or allowed. If you broke this rule, you'd be made fun of and called names.

The rule applies to every male. Even--or perhaps especially--the most successful sports stars. Take the first Bret Favre retirement speech as an example (the one from the Green Bay Packers, not from the New York Jets). He obviously had thought a lot about his decision to stop playing football, and he must have talked it through with his most trusted advisors. While he appeared to be comfortable with his decision, I'm willing to bet that it wasn't until he stepped onto that podium to make the announcement that the reality hit him. So he cried.

I wonder, how many of you guys laughed at him? How many of you and your friends said, "Did you watch Bret Favre cry like a baby? What a wimp." Better yet, how many of you said to yourself, *I would never pull a Bret Favre in front of my friends. No way!*

On the flip side, how many of your wives commented, "Wow! I have a lot of respect for him. For him to show his true emotions like that was very touching."

The same event, but two completely different reactions.

I saw the same differences when it came to the way Robin and I coped with our loss.

While I was reluctant to let my guard down and tell my male acquaintances how badly I was hurting for fear of being viewed as weak, my wife talked about her feelings with all her female friends whether they were that close to her or not.. She was more of an open book, while I stayed closed.

Guys, let me tell you, there's a tremendous advantage in "getting it out." I saw with my own eyes how my wife was able to move through the grieving stages with more ease, comfort and speed than I could, because she *talked* about it. I didn't.

When my golf league started up again for the first time after the death of Samantha, it quickly became clear to me that the guys in the league were more comfortable talking about the Red Sox than the feelings of a man who just lost his daughter. Rather than say, "How are you doing?" they simply didn't say anything at all. It was the proverbial elephant in the room. Everyone knew it was there, could feel it, could sense it, but no one ever said anything about it. I couldn't believe it.

For the first half of that season, I felt hurt and anger. I thought, *Screw these guys. I don't need or want to be friends with any of them. It's just a golf league, and it's an excuse for me to play golf every week. That's all it is.*

What I perceived as lack of caring left me with a very poor impression of humanity's ability to show compassion for someone like me. I spent many sessions with my bereavement counselor expressing my anger, disbelief and feelings of being alone on this journey, which I blamed partially on the lack of support I was getting from my golf buddies. I thought those guys were an insensitive bunch, and I came within inches of quitting the league because of that.

One day, in therapy, I said in anger, "These guys don't care about me. They never ask how I'm doing, or how Robin is, or anything else related to Samantha. Why? Why are they so cold?" I just didn't get it. It bothered me so much, and I couldn't figure out why they were treating me that way. While I didn't want any special treatment, I did expect them to check in every so often and ask how I was doing. Was that too much to ask?

Despite my resentment, my wife, father, and therapist talked me into sticking with the league. For one thing, it gave me an excuse to get out and play some golf every Tuesday, hang out with the guys, and take my mind off things. For another, the weekly play allowed me to improve my game, something I was interested in doing.

Eventually, I said to myself, *Let's do a test. I'll subtly mention how I'm feeling and see if anyone picks up on it. If nobody does, I'll know these guys don't care.*

Well, lo and behold, the first guy I subjected to this experiment said, "I've wanted to ask how you and your family are doing, but I didn't know what to say. I was afraid that if I said something to you, you'd start crying and I didn't want to do that to you. So, I didn't say anything." This opened the door and led us into a whole discussion on how I was feeling, how he would feel if he lost one of his kids, and what I was doing to cope. It was a great conversation, one that showed me that guys aren't as callous and uncaring as they seem; sometimes they just don't know what to say.

-   -   -

It took three years for me to learn how my golf buddies really felt, and when I did, it completely blew me away and caused *me* to cry like a baby.

One night several of the guys and I were hanging out after a round of golf, having a few beers and enjoying each other's company. At one point, I happened to share that the third anniversary of Samantha's death was coming up in a couple of weeks. This simple statement opened the floodgates for one guy in particular, who'd been wanting to share some information with me for some time but hadn't. He told me how all of the guys had rallied on my behalf and actually attended the funeral in support of me. He said they had arranged a caravan of three cars driving to the funeral and one car, in fact, had six guys crammed into it. Mind you, Samantha died just after midnight on Thursday and the funeral was around noon on Friday. Even though all the guys live in the same town, with such short notice I'm sure they had to rearrange their personal and job commitments to make the trip.

While I knew the guy sharing the story had been at the funeral, I had no idea that any of the others had attended. I thought he had gone as the sole representative of the league. Another guy with us that night told me that between the funeral and the start of the next season's golf league, the guys had private meetings at the club's bar to talk about my situation. "How should we treat Jon? What do we say to him? How do we make him feel comfortable? How do we show him our support?"

When I learned that these guys had done this for me, I was completely blown away. I had no idea that I had this level of support from a bunch of guys I was just starting to get to know. I asked them, "Why didn't you tell me this earlier? If I had known about the support you guys were giving me behind the scenes and the care you had for me, I would have moved through the initial bereavement period so much more easily and quickly."

By now, I'm sure you can guess how they answered. They literally said things like, "We're men. We didn't know what to say. We're not trained on this kind of thing. Unlike women, we don't have conversations about 'how are you feeling today'? We simply didn't know what to do or say."

What aggravated me and gave me even more drive to write this book was the belief that if these guys had read a book like this one, maybe…just maybe…they would have reached out and helped me when I truly needed it, when the death was still very raw and fresh.

The lesson here is, "They just don't know what to say." I think it's that simple. There's something you can do, though, to help your friends show their support while giving you a sense of control. When you're in social situations with people who know about your loss but don't seem comfortable, have the courage to say, "Don't feel weird around me. Just be yourself. If you start talking about a subject that I'm not comfortable with, I'll tell you. Don't walk on eggshells around me and don't give me any special treatment just because of my situation."

This little speech will eliminate much of the awkwardness and give them the green light they need--and want- to treat you just like one of the guys.

# HOW MANY KIDS DO YOU HAVE?

When you meet new people, you expect to be asked, "How many kids do you have?" For me, it's no longer a simple question with a simple answer. It's probably one of the most painful, gut wrenching questions I'm ever asked, causing me great discomfort coupled with a huge internal debate over how to answer. Do I want to tell the truth or do I want to make it easy for everyone?

Seriously, this is the debate I have in my head every time the question arises about how many children I have. As soon as I hear, "So... how many..." I know exactly where they're going and my first reaction is, *Oh no...What do I say?* If I'm with someone who knows me and my situation, I notice that they, too, cringe as the first words emerge. Many times, my friends will shoot me a glance that says, "Do you want me to handle this?" or "Sorry about that. Had I known they were going to ask that question, I would have told them not to."

Especially in the beginning, when I was still emotionally raw, this question would cause me to gasp, a most uncomfortable, knee-jerk physical reaction. If you're a guy, then you know how painful it is to get kicked in the groin. You immediately double over in pain and then fall to the ground, lying in the fetal position, waiting for the agony to go away. That's how I felt the first time someone asked me "the question." It was literally like a kick to the groin.

So, what's the right answer? To this day I still dread that question. Even though Samantha is not physically here, she is *still* my child and a part of me. I still ask myself "what do I say"? Do I tell the truth, and if I do, will that make the rest of our conversation incredibly awkward and uncomfortable?

Besides not wanting to hypothetically smack that person in the face with, "I don't know you but here's the deal, I lost a child recently," I also don't want to get bogged down with a load of other questions concerning the circumstances surrounding Samantha's death and how I handled it, either. The truth is, I'm still "handling" it and always will be.

During the first year or so, most of the time I answered the question with, "One child." The first few times I cried, but after about the tenth time, I was able to say it without any tears. While it turns my insides upside down, that simple answer usually makes things a lot easier and less complicated, not to mention that it avoids making the questioner feel they've put their foot in their mouth.

The first time I was hit with that question, I was on a sales call, so I didn't know any of the people on a personal basis. During the car ride to the meeting, I was more nervous about whether that question would be asked than about the meeting itself. I don't know why I was thinking about it, but I must have felt that being asked the question was a real possibility, or perhaps it was my anxiety revving up. Anyway, I made the decision that should it be asked, I'd provide my standard answer, "One child," because I didn't want anyone to feel sorry for me, which typically transitioned into a general awkwardness for everyone.

The car ride took forty-five minutes, and I spent the entire time psyching myself up for the anticipated question. I kept saying, "I have one child" over and over again to myself.

By the time I got to the meeting, I was feeling pretty drained. When I walked into the conference room, there were four people already there standing by the table facing me, chatting with one another. And sure enough, during the initial "getting to know you" chit chat, the dreaded question came up. My heart began pounding and my forehead started sweating, yet by some miracle I was able to blurt out the word "One" without shedding a tear. I kept my eyes focused on the table top, not daring to look directly into anyone's eyes for fear they might press the topic further. Thankfully, they didn't, although I'm sure they figured out that something was amiss.

For the most part, the meeting went pretty well. But when I got into my car before heading back to the office, I was struck with guilt. I actually said out loud, "I'm sorry Samantha. You know you're still my child. Don't think Daddy doesn't still love you." The feeling of guilt was such a powerful force at that moment that I cried my eyes out, right there in the parking garage. There would be no opportunity for me to make up for my answer with a hug and a kiss when I got home, because she wouldn't be there.

In certain business situations, I feel it's best to keep the conversation focused on the prospect's agenda. While it's not a clear-cut rule for me, in some instances it's perfectly appropriate for me to answer "two children" and then delve into the story a bit more, should I choose to do so. Basically, I take each situation as it comes and, depending on my mood, I often answer, "Two, but one passed away." I've noticed that I'm more inclined to answer in that manner to a woman than to a man. It must be another guy thing.

As the years go by, I struggle with this question a little less. It no longer rips my insides apart the way it used to, and the debate that rages in my head only lasts but a millisecond now.

-   -   -

As I look back on things, if I had to do it over again, I would have come up with a plan on how to answer the question for different social situations and I would have stuck to that plan when confronted with the challenge. Had I taken that approach,

I could have saved myself a lot of stress and anxiety.

If you have lost a child and struggle with this problem, I suggest setting up some rules for yourself. For example, if you're at a party and someone asks how many kids you have, you can comfortably respond that you have a child who's deceased. You could also answer, "We had two (or whatever the number is) but one passed away suddenly, so now we have one."

If people push for more details, it's okay for you to offer, "No offense, but I really don't want to go into the details about the whole situation right now." Believe me, people will be more than accommodating and will honor your request and respect you for setting this boundary. You'll be in a better position to manage your emotions by knowing how you're going to answer the question, and because you've set up the ground rules, you're in control of the depth of the conversation. Having that kind of control will give you the comfort you so desperately need.

If, on the other hand, you decide to answer, "One child," don't feel guilty. At this point, it's not about your deceased child, it's about you and what works best for you in a social or business situation. Answering in this way is not disrespectful of your deceased child, nor does it diminish any of your memories for that child. Instead, it's more about your coping skills, getting back into the game, re-engaging with the world, and learning how to be in social situations without having your heart beat a million times per second from a debilitating anxiety attack.

As the pain subsides, perhaps you'll create some new rules and be able to talk about it more opening and candidly. These new rules can be evaluated on your own sliding scale that's determined by your comfort level in that moment. The whole point of setting up rules is to make you feel comfortable and confident. You've been through an incredibly rough time, so when you finally go out, you deserve to enjoy yourself. So set up whatever rules work for you.

And remember, when you get back to your office after your business meeting, or back home after a party, give yourself a pat on the back for coming up with a plan and sticking to it. Doing so is a win/win--for you and for those around you. You've learned how to turn a potentially debilitating situation into one of comfort and ease. You made it. Be proud of yourself!

# PERSEVERING

# I HAVE A RESPONSIBILITY

When I was a kid, a family in our neighborhood lost their teenage son in a car accident. I used to clean their pool, so I had some interaction with them. Their son's death completely devastated the family, particularly the father. He had been a muscular, robust, successful entrepreneur; the type of guy others were drawn to, with his engaging personality and leadership aura. He owned several Dunkin Donuts franchises and he used to give away donuts to the kids in the neighborhood, especially me whenever I was at his home to clean the pool. It was understood that his son would take over the family business when he was old enough to do so.

Everything changed after the accident, and not just their plans for the future. The father changed physically. He began to shrivel up. Gone were his large forearms and strong back. He became extremely skinny and stood hunched over, and dragged his feet when he walked. His face became long and sullen and his skin took on an unhealthy ashen tone. He was no longer an energetic go-getter, and the twinkle that had always been in his eyes was gone.

He stopped talking to me unless he had to, and he ceased passing out donuts to the kids in the neighborhood. He didn't seem to care about anything anymore. It was as if the father had died. He also had a couple of daughters and I doubt very much that he was able to continue functioning as their father. While this all happened approximately thirty-five years ago, I can still clearly picture the change that took place in this man. I don't know what happened to the family because they moved away a few years after the boy's death.

Over the years, I have seen this happen to other people.

My company had a client whose wife was diagnosed with breast cancer. He was an entrepreneur who had built up a nice little ten-person information technology consulting business. His wife's illness devastated him to the point that he was not able to go in to work. I'd call to talk with him about the project he had hired us to do, yet could never reach him. The project, which was an important sales and marketing initiative for his company, dragged on forever. It was incredibly frustrating for me and for his team because all parties recognized the strategic value this project could deliver to his company. Mind you, this guy was the driving force of the group, so nothing got done while he was out.

I liked this man personally, but I found myself becoming angry with him. Why couldn't he deal with his personal life after working hours? Didn't he realize he had a responsibility to his employees and clients? Why was he letting his business that he'd worked so hard to build, fall apart around him?

When Samantha passed away, I thought of these people I had known, and I vowed I would not let the same thing happen to me. I can say now that I was successful, although it was not easy. How was I able to continue functioning, when many people are not? I think the biggest reason was that I forced myself to stay focused on my responsibilities: to my wife, my son, my business and my employees.

- - -

I returned to work exactly one week after Samantha's funeral. It was a Friday and the team invited me into the office to have pizza for lunch. I still vividly remember walking down the hallway to enter the office. I was *so* scared. My heart was pounding. I was sweating and my hands were shaking. Before going in, I went into the bathroom to collect myself and throw some cold water on my face. When I walked out, I bumped into my one of my business partners. I told him how scared I was and showed him my shaking hands. He said, "Do you want to go back home? You don't have to do this." I immediately said, "No! I *have* to do this. If I turn back now, it'll make returning to work for real that much harder." Trust me, it would have been much easier to avoid going in and returning to the comfort of my bed. But I knew, without even having to think about it, that taking that route would be the wrong choice.

When I walked in, everyone got up from their cubical and walked over to me. I remember the first thing I said to everyone: "Don't worry. I'm the same Jon. I'm just real sad." I said that because I wanted to assure them that I'd be okay. The last thing I wanted to have was a mass exodus of employees because they felt one of the owners wasn't capable of performing his job. I also didn't want them to treat me with kid gloves. I refused to be pitied.

The lunch ended up being great therapy and a confidence builder for me. I managed to get through it without breaking down or having an anxiety attack. We kept the topics light and everyone avoided the subject of Samantha's passing, which was fine with me. The anticipation was a lot worse than the actual event, and I remembered to give myself yet another "pat on the back" for a job well done when I got home.

As I eased back into work, there were many days I'd no sooner arrive at the office than I wanted to immediately drive back home. I was hurting so badly from Samantha's death and didn't need this added stress of having to deal with clients and trying to run a business. Believe me, there were many days when I almost did what that client whose wife was sick had done--withdraw and retreat. But the responsibility I felt I owed to the company and to the employees who had helped to make it successful, *always* kept my head in the game.

I was thankful for the effort our employees made and the commitment they had for the company. It was their effort, commitment, and expertise that had made the company grow. So how, in good consciousness, could I let them down by giving into my grief? And, more importantly, how could I do that to their families? What would happen to our employees' families if my company went belly-up because I couldn't deal with my grief? They had made a pledge to me and the company...didn't I owe them the same in return? Could I live with myself if I had given up on them and the company? The answer was a resounding "NO!"

-   -   -

Focusing on family responsibility was a different kind of challenge. I've already discussed my responsibility toward my son, Jake, throughout this book. In fact, it was first thing my mother talked to me about--that I had a responsibility to Jake not to let him lose that smile.

In this chapter, I want to talk about my responsibility to my wife, Robin. I realized that I wasn't the only one going through this horrific pain; after all, she was suffering too. It wouldn't be fair to her if I put myself into a cocoon and became unavailable for her. What would that do to our marriage?

In fact, many people said to us, "Don't let this heartbreak get in between you two. We'd hate to see this tragedy ruin your relationship and see you end up getting divorced." Robin's dad Mike also said this, as well as several of my closest friends. Apparently, and this is just anecdotal, many couples seem to get divorced after a tragedy like ours. I can think of several reasons why this would happen, including:

1.  They can't communicate or talk about the death, so both

drift apart and eventually go their own separate ways.

2. The loss is so painful that the house becomes dominated by doom and gloom; they hate going home.
3. They blame each other for the loss.
4. Being with that other person reinforces the loss; they feel there's no escape.
5. Other issues that existed prior to the loss become exacerbated.

One of the first things I said to Robin after Samantha's death was, "You don't have to worry about us. We will not drift apart or let this tragedy pull us apart. We owe it to each other and to Samantha and to Jake to get through this together. Go do your own grief work, but don't worry about me or us." I think saying that to her proved how strong we were as a couple and, as she dealt with her own grieving process, this was one less thing to be concerned about.

In my mind, if our marriage had broken up due to our loss, it would have been a second, brutal tragedy for Jake. I couldn't and wouldn't do that to him or Robin.

I'm not a marriage counselor, nor am I an expert on relationships, but if I had to share one bit of advice regarding your relationship with your spouse, it's this: keep the communication lines open. Check in with her as often as you feel she's comfortable having you do so. A simple "How are you doing today, honey?' or "You know I'm there for you. You can talk to me whenever you want" will go a long way in preserving and strengthening your marriage. Even if she never takes you up on it, don't worry--it's the gesture and intent that count.

In my case, I found that Robin was more open about her feelings with a few of her closest girlfriends than with me. I supported this whole heartedly, because the important thing was that she was talking about her emotions and wasn't holding them in. Just because she did this more often with her girlfriends than with me, didn't matter. I wanted her to express herself because that was the healthy way to address the loss.

Obviously, if there are underlying tensions that suddenly start boiling over, I recommend going to a marriage counselor to work through those issues. Make a conscious effort to reach out and be there for your spouse, and don't let problems fester and grow. Promise yourself that you won't let this loss cause even more suffering by destroying your family as well.

# STRENGTH AND COURAGE

How do you get through the day? How do you handle your loss? How do you continue on with your life?

These are all questions I'm asked and that I've often asked myself. The answer is, having dealt with our loss for close to three years now, I believe I have "Balls of Steel!" While that term may not be the most politically correct, it's worked well for me and that's what's important here.

Although I still struggle with occasional anxiety, I believe with all my heart that I do, indeed, have Balls of Steel. Having a tragedy such as this foisted upon me, I *had* to possess them. If *I can get through this, I can get through anything!* is what I would say to myself, because I knew it was exactly that kind of stamina I needed to see me through. This mindset, and the realization that I had Balls of Steel, enabled me to resume functioning as a healthy adult.

What exactly does Balls of Steel mean? For me, it means strength. Strength to get through a catastrophe, such as losing a child and not letting it take over, defeat you and ultimately destroy all you've worked for in your life. It's the strength needed to allow yourself to think, remember and talk about your deceased child. To keep her memory alive without having it obliterate you, all at the same time. To act as your own motivational coach and frequently, to give yourself a pep talk: "*I'm going to do all the hard, painful grief work so that I can get to the other side in one piece!*"

Fundamentally, Balls of Steel means that I chose to continue to live life with a positive attitude. Thanks to my Balls of Steel, I can now get out of bed in the morning, take my shower, eat breakfast and get out the door in a positive frame of mind--*I'm alive! That's a good thing. I am going to do my best today. I am going to have a good day.* Granted, after suffering the most devastating kind of loss there is, just getting out of bed qualifies you as having Balls of Steel. However, it's all the better if you can use that same strength to create other positive things throughout your daily agenda.

Balls of Steel means recognizing that life is forever altered in such a way that only another parent who's lost a child can understand. While life will be different, it doesn't mean that it needs to be a horrible existence. Knowing this, and deciding to continue to live life to the fullest, is what having Balls of Steel is all about.

Now, I'm not suggesting you do something crazy like skydiving or any other testosterone-laden stunt. I'm just saying that being able to laugh, smile and be happy are the unsung vital elements to acquiring Balls of Steel. If you do nothing else but those three things, congratulations--you still qualify as having Balls of Steel.

Basically, you're telling the grief, depression, and unspeakable pain, "I'm not going to let you ruin my life. I'm not going to let you dictate how I'm going to live." You're taking a stand and saying "No!" to the powerfully enticing temptation to misuse drugs and alcohol, or to take the ultimate "out" by committing suicide.

The concept is not all about being tough. It also means not being afraid to love someone, despite your loss. My daughter was taken away from me without any advance notice and I easily could have used that as an excuse to recoil from intimate relationships as emotional protection. But instead, I chose to continue my adoration towards the people who are important in my life. I didn't disengage from feeling or withdraw from any emotional interaction with others, because then I'd be no better than a mechanical robot. I decided not to do that to myself or to anyone else that matters to me. I plan on living for a long time and find no value in believing I can block out any future pain by ignoring feelings of love.

Living through this experience, I recognized the importance of building healthy, nurturing relationships and, most significantly, maintaining them when things go horribly wrong. You really don't have the luxury of crawling into a shell from which you may never emerge.

Balls of Steel also means having courage. Courage is a key mindset to allow you to embrace and fulfill your responsibilities. You need to look the pain you're feeling in the face and say, "Screw you!" You need to declare to the anxiety that hovers nearby and waits to overtake you, "I'm going to beat you!"

Acquiring Balls of Steel provides you with the necessary tools you need in getting through something few people are capable of surviving. Look around you. If the couple standing next to you suddenly lost a child, how well do you feel they'd handle it, or would they be helpless and simply crumble under the severe stress? I've made it this far. I've decided to lead as normal a life as possible despite the hole in my heart. *That's* having Balls of Steel!

The phrase applies to all the little things in your life, as well as the big things. It means challenging yourself to keep every appointment with your bereavement counselor, no matter how lousy you're feeling and, once you get there, to not hold anything back.

It requires you to look at the pictures of your deceased child and remember him or her during happier times, not at the point of his/her death. It means having the mental muscle to say, "I'm not going there. Instead, I'm going to pick a memory that gives me great joy and, rather than feeling beaten up when I'm done, I'm going to feel pretty good. Not necessarily happy, but not devastated, either."

The notion of having Balls of Steel can get you through those days when you just want to give up, stop the fight and pick up that bottle of vodka, or take that handful of "happy pills" to ease the pain. We all have a tipping point, but having Balls of Steel won't let you make a habit out of it.

Balls of Steel requires having patience. I'm going to be totally honest here: you won't get there overnight. It took me almost three years before I began to recognize the concept and incorporate it into my life. But the point is, it doesn't matter how long it takes; it's getting there and recognizing that you've arrived that's important, even if it's ten years after the death of your child.

-   -   -

How do you get there? One key is to recognize your wins, no matter how small they are. Tell yourself, "Job well done" for every single accomplishment you achieve during the entire grieving process.

As I mentioned before, one of the simplest of my early wins was being able to look at Samantha's pictures as I walked downstairs first thing in the morning, and not throwing up. Getting to the bottom of the stairs "in one piece" was a win and I congratulated myself every day I did it. For every such win, large or small, say to yourself, *Congratulations! You looked at the photos, even if it was for a second or two. That took guts.* And on days when you can't handle it, refuse to beat yourself up. It takes Balls of Steels to forgive yourself and not say negative things like *You wimp. You couldn't even look at your daughter's pictures. What kind of a man are you?*

The reason for the back patting is twofold. First, you're acknowledging to yourself, *I can do this*. Second, and better yet, is the fact that you did it! It's a confidence builder. The more you take stock of your accomplishments, the more strength you'll have to get through the next challenge and the better you'll feel about it all. You'll recognize how you're taking control.

You want to know another way to get there? Open up. Ask your guy friends for support. Tell them how you're hurting and that you need their help. Seeing them come around will give you the utmost confidence that you have a team of guys there to support you, and now you won't feel so all alone. Believe me, feeling that you're all alone as you fight to get through the bereavement process is an incredibly scary thing. Who in their right mind would ever want to go through this at all, let alone by themselves? If you only talk about what you're going through once a week or so to your bereavement counselor, do you really think that's enough time and attention to the topic for you to get through it successfully? Think about it; talking about the death of your child at a one-hour, once-a-week therapy session isn't enough. The topic needs more "air time."

I'm not suggesting going overboard and talking about your feelings every time you go out socially with your buddies. That's overkill, so use your best judgment. Know when it's the right time and place to broach the subject. The same holds true with your wife. Although she's your life's partner and your best friend, don't make your pain the constant topic of conversation. She's going through the same emotional torture, and your tendency to focus on only *your* feelings can get old really fast and will surely put a strain on your relationship.

Based on my experience, this seemingly easy action of showing some weakness to your guy friends is actually one of the hardest things to do. I've said this before--it's not in the male DNA to do this, so it's going to feel awkward and intimidating at first. True, you run the risk of not getting any support and some guys may even express, "I can't handle this. I don't want to talk about this with you," but the chances of that happening are pretty remote.

Think about it. If one of your guy friends came to you and was in emotional pain due to a loss of someone close to him and asked for your support, would you turn him down, or would you do whatever it took to help him navigate through his grief? You know exactly what you'd do and you have to trust that he'd do the same for you.

- - -

It's so easy to go down the path of drinking your pain and anxiety away. Believe me, I know because I came close to choosing that route. Getting drunk and having a few moments of peace sure sounded like a life-saver when I was going through such unbearable pain in the raw period after Samantha died. But that route is the antithesis of Balls of Steel. It's taking the easy way out because, rather than facing your grief and working to get through it, you're avoiding that hard work by making yourself feel better temporarily.

I know a guy who did choose that route. His wife told me that when they tragically lost their young son, at first he seemed to continue to be a hard working, responsible, young guy with a business, and with two surviving kids. Then he fell into a downward spiral and was never able to fully recover. For the first two years or so, he just sat in a chair on their front lawn, watching the two surviving kids play while downing bottles of whiskey. Eventually, he stopped working all together, and lost his business and his lust for life. He also began to suffer various health issues, like a bad back, and other ailments that he'd never had before. In a nutshell, life became too much for him.

Over time, he finally got a little better, returned to work

and rejuvenated his passion for life, and even fathered two more kids. Unfortunately, the drinking never left him. He had become a full blown alcoholic.

I met him about ten years after the death of his child and my recollection of him was that he was a "sad sack." I could look into his eyes and see the hurt and the pain, which for him was as alive and fresh as when it happened so many years ago.

One of the first things I did, when I was first tempted to drink large quantities of alcohol, was to remind myself of this man and silently ask myself, *Do I want to become like him? Is this the path I truly want to take; one littered with unfulfilled dreams, a life of misery and poor health? Absolutely not!*

Although I'm sorry for his pain, I'm glad I had him as an example of what *not* to do. I might not have been able to avoid that route had I not seen, firsthand, the destruction brought about by his actions and how they directly affected his loved ones.

So, to achieve Balls of Steel, my advice to you is to hit grief head on and don't mask it with alcohol or drugs. The grief won't be denied. It won't go away by not talking about it or trying to convince yourself that you're okay. But as strong as the grief is, it is not as strong as Balls of Steel. You can refuse to give in. You can refuse to become like the guy who succumbed to alcoholism, wasted his life, and hurt his marriage and his relationship with his surviving kids.

If you can use the idea of Balls of Steel to conjure up a sense of strength, then use it – frequently! You've been through unspeakable pain and you can bank on more to come, so do whatever it takes to keep on track and continue progressing through your grief. Find your Balls of Steel and make them work for *YOU!*

# LOVE IS THE ANSWER

If you asked me, "What helped you get through the grieving process?" or "How did you successfully make it to the other side?" I'd have to say it's the love I have for my son Jake. This deep love, which goes to my very core, functioned as a counterbalance to the gut-wrenching pain when Samantha first passed away, and it's still my source of strength, especially for the tough times like her birthday and the anniversary of her death.

This love was like a massive, strong concrete wall I could lean my back against and count on to shore me up whenever the Heavy Wet Blanket feeling of depression hit me. It gave me strength and enabled me to "turn the tables" on the depression, allowing me to switch my focus from the horrible pain of the loss of my daughter, to the more exuberant feeling of love I have for my son.

To put it more succinctly, the love I have for Jake and the wonderful feeling this love gave me was like a safe haven, a security blanket of sorts. I knew that no matter how low I felt, if I started concentrating on the love I felt for Jake, I would slowly begin to feel better. It might take me a couple of weeks to emerge from that hell, but if I kept concentrating and feeling the love, I knew I'd eventually come around. This love was the equivalent of my "happy pill."

I determined that it was imperative for Jake to know that despite losing Samantha, he always had his mommy and daddy. I wanted him to know that no matter what, he always had our unconditional love.

Every day I make it a point to say to him first thing in the morning, "I love you Jake." If there's one thing in the world that I don't want him to have any doubts about, it's the love I have for him. I feel his awareness of this deep devotion will give him confidence in life because he'll know that I'll always there for him and that he can always count on me for anything.

The winter of Samantha's death, I took Jake swimming every weekend--it was our special time together and immediately became something we both looked forward to very much. We talked with enthusiasm about going swimming together, how we'd have races with one another, and how much Jake enjoyed showing me his newly learned swimming strokes and his latest cannonball jump.

When Saturday rolled around, Jake would get up at the crack of dawn and come running into our bedroom asking, "When are we going swimming, Daddy?" It was such a joy to see him so excited and acting like a normal little boy so soon after Samantha's death.

The swimming was good therapy for both of us because we got to spend quality time with one another. It was an hour or two of pure joy, fun, and happiness, plus it provided me with a much needed break from the constant pain and misery I felt.

Throwing Jake up in the air in the pool, and hearing him laugh and seeing him have a great time, made me feel wonderful. And even though the feeling only lasted an hour or so, it was "just what the doctor ordered." It was invigorating and made me feel "alive" again, a feeling I sorely missed and rarely felt that first year after Samantha's death.

More than just having some fun together, I wanted Jake to know that no matter what the circumstances were, no matter how depressed or pained I felt, his daddy would always be there for him and that he was always my top priority. Given our goal of having Jake emerge from all this unshaken and unchanged, I felt it vital to deliver this message to him through my actions. I hoped that my focused commitment to him would be the catalyst he needed to boost his confidence so that he could tackle any adversity life threw his way.

Because we wanted Jake to get back to his routine as quickly as possible, we took him back to school the next Monday, which was only three days after the funeral. We also continued to take him to his weekly Saturday play date for little kids at a local gym, which began the weekend following the funeral.

Making the decision to get Jake back to his normal routine as quickly as possible was a tough one. Emotionally, it would have been a lot easier for Robin and me if we could have stretched the time frame a little bit longer for our grieving period. But, again, we felt it best for Jake's mental and emotional health to get him back on track as quickly as possible.

To this day, whenever I feel sad or I think about how much I miss Samantha, I turn my thoughts to how much love I feel for Jake along with the warmth that love brings to me, and I immediately feel healthier. It's like a drug for me. I know how good it feels and I want to feel it all the time. In all honesty, without Jake's love to fall back on, I don't think I could have made it through Samantha's passing - and that's the truth.

Perhaps you don't have another child on whom to focus your love, in which case your loss is all the harder. But the lesson is still the same: find someone to love, whether it's your wife or your sibling or your closest friend. That love will help to pull you through, I guarantee it. Love really is the answer.

# SHOULD WE HAVE
# MORE KIDS?

# READY AT LAST

From the time Samantha passed away, we knew we wanted to have more kids. In fact, when we got married we originally planned on having three kids: two close together and a third a little later on.

Robin and I are no "spring chickens." I was forty-one when Samantha died and Robin was thirty-nine. Although time was of the essence because Robin's "biological clock" was ticking, for the first year or so after Samantha's passing, we didn't discuss having other children out of respect to Samantha. We both thought: *How can we even think about having other kids when her grave isn't even cold yet? Don't we owe it to Samantha to grieve for a period of time? How can we immediately turn around and have other kids? Don't we need to go through the grieving process first? Don't we have to "repair" ourselves before we can think of caring for another person?* To do otherwise, I felt, wouldn't be fair to me or to the new child.

Plus, how would Jake react to a new baby so quickly after Samantha's passing? Wouldn't that confuse him and dilute the memories he had of his baby sister? For these and many other reasons, we decided to take our time before having another child.

One of my biggest fears was whether I still had it in me to *love* another child. Could I conceivably muster up that emotion again, or was I too emotionally drained from experiencing Samantha's death? Would I feel guilty for loving another child? Would I feel that I had abandoned Samantha's memory? Would she be forgotten?

Given my emotional condition, I had serious doubts

about my ability to be a good father to another child. I was having enough trouble keeping myself together, never mind being the father to a newborn. Would I be able to even hold a baby again? How weird would that be? Could I give myself completely to another human being, especially a baby who's so needy? Did I have anything left to give another life?

I realized that if we were to have another child, I needed to be fully engaged. I needed to be capable of giving this child all the love, support and nourishment I gave to Samantha and continue to give to Jake. If I couldn't do that, I would have failed as a parent, especially to this new child. It was my duty to provide this child with the best opportunity to grow into a contributing adult who adds value to society, and most importantly, feels valued himself. By having the ability to love this child unconditionally, while providing a supportive and loving home, I would give this child the confidence he or she would need to grow up healthy and have the best shot at a successful life.

More to the point, I needed to be strong enough to *not* compare this child to Samantha. In no way did I want this child to think that we were trying to replace Samantha. Our new child, if we had one, needed to know and feel, without any question, that we wanted him or her for the pure reason of bringing another human being into our family to love.

-  -  -

A year went by with these thoughts in my mind, and I still was not ready to have another child. The doubts wouldn't go away. The reality was, I still could barely look at little girls, let alone pick up and hold one, and there I was considering having another child? Was I crazy?

This debate raged in my mind. It also was the topic of

many conversations with Robin. Finally, sometime between the first and second anniversary of Samantha's passing, I started talking with my bereavement counselor about whether to have another child. The thought scared the living daylights out of me. The paranoia went on: *What if the child wasn't healthy? What if there was a problem with the pregnancy? What if the child was born healthy, but got sick later on, like Samantha did?*

I literally drove myself bananas, to the point where I had trouble "performing." Every time Robin would even mention trying, anxiety would hit: *Oh my gosh! She wants to have another baby. I couldn't handle it if something was wrong with the child.* The result was, whenever Robin came into our bedroom, I'd lie there pretending to be asleep, all the while my heart pounding in fear. *Please don't make me wake up and try to make a baby. I'm not ready. I can't handle the stress.* All I could envision was being totally stressed out for the entire nine months, constantly worrying about whether the baby would be born healthy.

Yet at the same time, I knew I wanted another child, not just for me but for Robin and Jake, too. Jake missed his baby sister and often said to us, "I want to be a big brudder again," as he would pronounce the word.

There were times, such as coming home from one of his friend's birthday parties, when he'd ask, "How come I can't have a baby sister?" It broke our hearts. Even at four years old and in the early phases of being able to fully communicate, he cut to the chase and found a way to tell us how much he missed Samantha.

Believe me, I was feeling the pressure. And not just from Robin and Jake, but from my parents, too. "You're not getting any younger and neither is Robin", they'd say. My friends also began asking me about our plans for having another child.

"Am I being a wimp for not feeling like I'm able to

handle having another child?" I'd ask my bereavement counselor. "Of course not", he'd say. "Look at what you've been through. Any normal person would have misgivings and be fearful."

What scared me the most was the sense of a lack of control. As you know, when you're expecting a child, you don't have a heck of a lot of control over anything. Sure, your wife can take pre-natal vitamins and watch what she eats, but the truth remains that you really have no control over the outcome. Some of my worst thoughts were, *If this child is born unhealthy, I'm either going to commit suicide, freak out, or end up in a mental hospital.* I truly believed this.

I didn't want to tell Robin of my fears right away, because I didn't want to disappoint her, and I had no clue about how to properly broach the subject. Remember, this level of anxiety was new to me, so I really didn't know how to describe it to her.

My bereavement counselor and I decided to focus on how to get me "ready" to have another child. We explored my fears in depth, discussed the worst case scenario, and the odds of something like that happening a second time. That was the burning question for me: *Was Samantha's death an anomaly, or was it something that could happen to our next child?* I had to know, or at least find an answer I could accept, for my own sanity.

I often said to myself and to my bereavement counselor, *"I'm hurting. I can barely take care of myself. How in the world am I going to be able to give wholeheartedly to another human being? I'm giving 100% of my energy to myself because I want to successfully get through this grieving process. I want to come out on the other side as a fully functioning, emotionally healthy adult and an engaging father and husband. How can I do that along with giving love to a new baby right now?"*

The answer was crystal clear: I couldn't. There's only so much "gas in the tank." If I'm using up 100% of my energy doing the tough grief work, how in the world can I have anything left to give to a newborn? I knew I wasn't ready and, quite frankly, feared whether I'd *ever* be ready.

- - -

After several sessions with my bereavement counselor, I finally had the strength to tell Robin the truth. I told her how I'd been faking being asleep and why. I came clean about my all my fears. Let me tell you, doing so made me feel so much better. No longer did I have to hide it from her. Instead, I could now keep her in the loop on my progress. I felt comfortable letting her in, knowing that she wasn't going to resent me or think I was being selfish.

Once I divulged my fears, I actually started feeling healthier. Robin didn't pressure me and was totally understanding and supportive. To ease my fears about the chances of having a child with some horrible disease, we went to a geneticist and were both tested for several types of known illnesses and defects. I was concerned about whether Samantha's death had something to do with our genetic combination. Thankfully, this doctor completely confirmed that genetics had absolutely nothing to do with Samantha's sudden illness and ultimate death. So, I was able to cross out that concern.

Robin also spoke with her OB/GYN who confirmed that Samantha's death was an anomaly and that the chances of something like that happening again were incredibly slim. She assured Robin that she would be closely monitored during every phase of the pregnancy, so the chances of something slipping by undetected would be highly unlikely.

I took a full physical exam, which confirmed that my health was excellent. I was beginning to regain control, which made me feel so much stronger, mentally as well as physically. I still wasn't thrilled about having another child, but at least I was getting closer.

Have you ever stood on a dock or the side of a pool, wanting to jump into the water, but dreading the shock of cold water you know will hit you? There you are, poised to jump, but unable to move. That's how I felt about taking that plunge and having another child. While I was ready to jump in with both feet, I felt stuck in mid-air; something still held me back, keeping me suspended in a state of limbo.

My bereavement counselor and I continued to talk about it. "You never know whether you're ready until you try," he'd say, and I knew he was right. But I *still* wasn't ready. For at least two or three months, I couldn't lose that feeling of "one foot in and one foot out."

Then one miraculous day, almost two years after Samantha passed away, I felt ready. I was watching Robin interact with a little girl around Samantha's age. You should have seen the joy in Robin's face. It was clear she was thinking about Samantha while playing with that little girl. Maybe she was fantasizing that the girl *was* Samantha. I don't know. All I saw was the look on Robin's face, her amazing smile. And then I thought about Jake and how much fun he and his baby sister had together. So I said to myself, *Okay Jon, how can you deny Robin that joy? How can you deny Jake that wonderful experience of being a big brother again?* It was a no brainer from that point on.

Fortunately, on the day that I had this epiphany, I had a meeting with my bereavement counselor. I told him about this episode and he said, "Jon, that's very noble of you, but you need to do this for *you*. Do you want another child? Do you feel ready?" This time, I didn't hesitate when I said, "Yes!"

We continued talking, especially about my lack of control issues. I'm sure I surprised him when I announced, "If there's something wrong with the child, I'll deal with it." Now I truly knew I was ready. I had had to make peace with that conclusion before I was able to commit to having another child. I had to *know*, unequivocally, that I could handle anything; otherwise I wasn't going to put myself, or anyone else, in that situation.

The counselor did his job by challenging me, saying, "You're volunteering to put yourself in a vulnerable position, a position where you have no control. How do you think that posture will impact your anxiety levels? On the flip side, as we've discussed and as you've come to realize due to your independent research, the likelihood of having a baby with a health issue is pretty remote. However it's there, nonetheless."

"You're right", I said. "Let me think about it before I tell Robin of my decision."

A week passed and I still felt comfortable with my decision. Oddly enough, I felt at ease the entire week. Yet another week went by and I still felt the same. The raging debate that had gone on in my head about having another child had ended. It was gone! And in its place--there was peace. Finally, I knew I was ready!

Approximately two weeks after my epiphany, I came home after work and said to Robin excitedly, "I'm ready to have another child!" That night, we began trying. With Jake and Samantha, Robin had gotten pregnant very easily and quickly, so of course we anticipated having the same luck this time around. One thing we didn't take into account was how Samantha's death and the stress it caused us, both mentally and physically, would impact our ability to get pregnant. Therefore, we shouldn't have been surprised to find that we weren't as fortunate this time.

Between the second and third year after Samantha died, we tried to get pregnant at every ovulation period. A few days later Robin would bring a home pregnancy test. We were definitely on a mission to expand our family again.

During that time, Robin got pregnant twice but neither pregnancy took. Both resulted in miscarriages. The first miscarriage was rough mentally because we'd never had one before, and it was a loss on the heels of an even bigger loss. We asked ourselves, *Does this mean we'll never be able to get pregnant?* This possibility was hard to accept, because once you decide to have kids, you don't want to take "No" for an answer.

The second miscarriage was even more devastating as the fetus was actually a baby. We knew we were pregnant, for Robin could feel the changes in her body, which were very similar to those that occurred when she was pregnant with Jake and Samantha. We were psyched; we were having another child!

Unfortunately, when Robin went for her scheduled ultrasound, the doctor informed her that the fetus had died. Its heart had stopped beating. Poor Robin. There she sat in the doctor's office expecting to be told "you're having a girl" and instead she's told the baby is dead. In fact, this appointment was supposed to be so routine that she told me I didn't need to accompany her. Thankfully, my mother was free that day, so she met Robin at the doctor's office and was there with her when this devastating news was delivered.

For Robin, the news of this baby's death was like reliving Samantha's. She was a basket case. For about two weeks she reverted back to September 14, 2006, the date of Samantha's death. It was awful seeing my wife in that much pain. Fortunately, Robin's a strong person and she was able to get it together in a couple of weeks with the help of her bereavement counselor.

After these two episodes, we concluded that having a child naturally wasn't in the cards for us. We couldn't handle another loss, so we gave up on trying to have a child the natural way.

The next option was Invitro Fertilization (IVF). We went to a fertility clinic and, even though we both passed our fertility tests, we decided against that route, as well. The doctor told us that at our age, we only had something like a 20% chance of actually giving birth. Once again, the odds seemed stacked against us. With odds that low, we couldn't emotionally handle a third loss. Therefore, we decided that IVF wasn't the right path for us, either.

# DECIDING TO ADOPT

All during this time, somewhere in the background, we'd been casually talking about the possibility of adoption. I remember having a conversation with Robin, maybe less than a year after Samantha's death, and saying something like, "Wouldn't it be a nice tribute to Samantha to adopt a child, to take an unwanted baby and give it love and a home? Wouldn't we be giving back and doing a good deed by adopting a child and bringing that child into a loving home?"

This theme of "a nice tribute to Samantha" grew and became something we began to believe in. We knew that Samantha would embrace our doing something like that, giving a child who wasn't wanted or who couldn't be supported by its birth parents, the love and devotion we gave her. That would be a nice, honorable thing to do: turn a tragedy into a blessed, positive thing.

While we were still trying to get pregnant, we attended a day long "Adoption 101" course, but truthfully, this option was still a distant one because we thought that we'd be able to have a biological child. It wasn't until the first miscarriage that we started talking seriously about adopting a baby. And once the second miscarriage occurred, we kicked the adoption mode into high gear.

The process was very thorough, requiring lots of government forms and applications. A social worker come to our home to interview us and evaluate the condition of our living environment. We had to have several friends write letters of recommendation and then we were required to go down to our police station to have our fingerprints taken and submitted to the FBI. Also, our local county and state police did background checks on us, along with our state's Department of Youth Services.

The most difficult part, from an emotional perspective, was putting together the booklet that explained why we wanted to adopt, along with a pictorial description of our family. This booklet would be used by the adoption agencies to "pitch" us to their birth mothers, and it was the only thing the birth mother had to go on when making her decision as to which family to choose. We hoped that our story would strike a chord with the birth mother and cause her to pick us instead of the other families.

Robin spent several days putting together our first booklet. The feedback from the agency was that it was too "Samantha focused." Talk about a punch in the gut. Here we were, trying to tell the story of our family, thinking we'd put together an awesome pictorial history and then we were told, "You need to take out a bunch of the photos of Samantha. A birth mother will look at your book, conclude that there's no way that her baby can hold a candle to Samantha, and end up picking someone else."

This feedback hurt Robin more than me. I said, "We want a baby, so whatever it takes to make a match is what we have to do."

Robin said, "This is my little baby girl they're talking about. She's still a member of the family even though she's not here physically. How can I just delete her from the book?"

After much debate, we decided to follow the feedback from the adoption agency. While it hurt, we had to "keep our eyes on the prize," and if fewer photos of Samantha would get us to our goal, then so be it.

- - -

The worst part about the adoption process is the waiting. You wait and wait and wait. There's nothing you can do about it. It's completely out of your control. We are still waiting as I write this.

People often ask, "How do you feel about having another baby?" I answer by saying this new baby will give me the chance to feel uncontainable joy and to feel passionate about something again-- two emotions I haven't felt in nearly three years. I'm ecstatic about feeling human again, to experience highs as well as lows, to have some balance in my life.

I want to clarify something here. In no way am I suggesting that the decision to adopt a child was for the sole purpose of making *me* feel better. That is *no*t the child's "job". I wanted a child, period! I wanted to hold, love and raise a child. I wanted this so much that I was even looking forward to changing its dirty diapers. Go figure!

Am I nervous? I am certainly conflicted. On the one hand, I'm scared because it's been nearly three years since I've held a baby, and having a newborn in our home will change our lives. Yet I'm so excited. I can't wait to bring a baby home.

Adoption provides another chance to cherish and raise a child and see him or her grow into a wonderful adult. When Samantha died, I felt cheated. Everything I had planned to do with her was ripped away from me before we had had the opportunity to experience those plans. It was gone before it even started. She had her whole life ahead of her, and even though she's dead and no longer feels anything, I still think she too got cheated. Once the adoption is finalized, I will have the opportunity to live those dreams again with this new life and see them through to fruition.

There will be life again in our house.

# EPILOGUE

I'm happy to share that Robin, Jake, Samantha and I are so very pleased to announce the arrival of Aiden Samuel into our lives. His middle name is a tribute to Samantha. He was born on February 17, 2010 and was officially adopted into our family two weeks later. After much soul searching and a few bumps along the way, we are blessed to add this bundle of pure love into our home and into our hearts.

# APPENDIX:
# MY PHASES OF THE
# GRIEVING PROCESS

Psychiatrists and grief experts have theories about the grieving process. They talk about the different phases and what you can expect and what you should do during each phase. But I have to ask, *How do they know how to get through it, if they've never personally experienced the death of a child?* After all, this isn't some textbook academic exercise.

Each person's grieving process is unique to them and may certainly differ from mine. But what the messages in this book bring to the table are firsthand accountings, written by me, a guy who went through it and, quite frankly, is still going through it. You may disagree with my choices and the path I took, but this story is "the real deal." To be honest, there's no perfect answer on how to deal with this type of tragedy. There are simply too many variables.

You may ask yourself, "What *are* the classic phases of the grieving process? How do I *know* I'm progressing and moving forward? What *can* I expect next?" I asked those very same questions, and I have to tell you that not knowing what was waiting for me around the corner contributed to my anxiety, big time! It was another example of not feeling in control and lacking the knowledge for navigating my way through the bereavement process.

I'm providing this appendix to share my own evolutionary process through grief. Remember, each phase doesn't necessarily end before the next one begins. Not everyone's journey will follow the exact sequence that mine did.

And let me repeat, I am not a psychiatrist or trained grief counselor. However, I think most men, and possibly women too, will experience similar phases in varying degrees.

For me, the grieving process followed two broad phases--the downward spiral, and the climb back to recovery.

# THE DOWNWARD SPIRAL

### INITIAL SHOCK

I'm at the hospital telling the doctors to stop life support. Am I really here?  Is this actually happening?  Wasn't Samantha dancing in her room just a few hours ago?  Is this just a dream? When am I going to wake up from this nightmare?

### DISBELIEF

I can't believe my baby is dead.  I can't believe that she's not going to be here any longer.  Can this be true?  Did it really happen?  Is it true that she'll never greet me when I come home from work?

### THE PAIN BEGINS

It's really true…she is dead.  She's not here anymore. I've hit rock bottom.  I'm in an emotional hole, the depths of which I never knew existed.  Can the human mind sink this low? Where's the bottom?  I've never been in this much pain in my life!  Will it ever end?  Is this how life will be for the remainder of my time?  I'm in so much pain that I'll do anything to make it go away.

### THE "WHY?" PHASE

Why me?  Why Samantha?  What did she do to deserve this?  Why did Jake have to lose his best friend?  Why us?  Why Robin?  Why do you get to lead a normal life while I don't?

### BITTERNESS

Everyone can just leave me alone!  All you have to worry about are the trivial day-to-day things.  Want a taste of my world? If you had to deal with what I'm dealing with, how many of you could handle it?

Look at you--you self absorbed happy go lucky people. Look at me--I'm miserable. I hate you all because you're happy. Here I am going through hell but you don't hear me complaining about it. I'd give anything to just have your issues to deal with. I have to cope with those AND with the death of my baby. How would you like to deal with that? You drop off your kids at preschool. You go to the gym. You sit around at Starbuck's talking with your friends and have the nerve to complain about life? How dare you! Look at what I'm dealing with. I wonder whether any of you could deal with what I'm going through.

## SCARLET LETTER

Everyone's staring at me. They're all talking about me. Wherever I go, everyone knows "that's the guy who lost his child." I feel like an outcast. Nobody asks me how I'm doing. Nobody cares. I'm all alone…

## ANXIETY

I'm afraid of my own shadow. Something bad and unexpected could happen at any time, now. I have no control over anything anymore!

How am I going to react when someone asks me how I'm doing? I can't handle social settings because they're too stressful. I'm staying home.

## HITTING BOTTOM

I'm so depressed. I don't know how I'm going to be able to function. Can it get any worse than this? Nothing in my life has prepared me for this. What's the game plan? How do I get through this in one piece?

- - -

The different phases of the "downward spiral" hit me in waves, and I believe they will come at most people this way. They just come at you, relentlessly, and there's nothing you can do about it.

Fortunately, this changes. Eventually you will hit bottom, and then you will have choices again. That is when you can begin the road back.

# THE ROAD BACK

Recovery begins when you admit your child has died, when you reach the realization that your child is no longer physically here. Once you've accepted that fact, you can begin the healing process. I'm not saying you need to "accept" the fact that your child has died. Anyone who has an ounce of compassion in their body would never espouse "accepting" the death of a child, because you simply can't. What I am saying is, recognize, realize and FEEL the death, and acknowledge with 100% conviction and certainty that your child will not be coming home. Once that declaration becomes your reality, you'll be better able to move through the various evolutions in the grieving process.

Anger, denial, and asking "Why?" muddies the situation and prohibits you from doing the tough but necessary grief work. You also have to fully comprehend how things will never be the same again. You'll be a different person; no question about it. At your core, you'll still be the same, but in some unexplained way, you'll be and feel "different." In my case, bouts of sadness and frequent anxiety were my new reality.

## IN-DEPTH RETROSPECTION AND REFLECTION

This phase follows closely on the heels of the certainty that the death has actually occurred. If you decide to go to counseling, make the commitment not to hold anything back. You will uncover things in your past that are contributing to your current feelings and the ways in which you deal with your loss. Example: I learned through my sessions with my grief counselor that I always had an issue with anxiety. It was always there, but never as "vocal" as it was once Samantha passed away. So, we explored my childhood and these feelings of anxiety in an effort to try to understand where they came from and why. Once I did that work, I was able to correct my current thinking and behavior, which enabled me to "quiet" those anxious episodes.

## DISCOVERY

If talking about your grief leads you down another path, let's say an episode in your life that's been subconsciously bugging you, go with it. Explore it. Understand it. Trust me, the severity of the emotions stirred up by your loss will force other feelings and memories that are lurking below the surface to rear their ugly heads. Everything comes gushing out, just like a volcano. I hope you're one of the lucky few who don't experience this, but if I'm an example of a pretty normal guy, then I'll bet you, too, may find other things that need exploration. If you want to get better, you need to confront these hidden emotions.

## EVOLUTION – ONE FOOT IN FRONT OF THE OTHER

As you go through each evolution, remember to give yourself a "pat on the back" for a job well done. These evolutions can be gut wrenching, so getting through them in one piece is cause for self-admiration.

Recognizing that you've "passed" a tough evolution gives you confidence that you'll continue to do well as you encounter more. Acknowledging your victories will also help to avoid any anticipatory anxiety. In preparation for challenging situations, such as visiting your child's grave site for the first time after the funeral, admit to yourself that the last step you took was tough. I was terribly frightened about it, but I passed with flying colors. Once you do, you'll have set yourself up for future success with any subsequent challenges.

## BALLS OF STEEL

Eventually, after your string of successes, you'll come to believe that you actually have "Balls of Steel." As a matter of fact, that's how I feel about myself today. It's my way of saying, "I've been through hell and now I'm back. Despite this tragic loss, I'm functioning as a normal, successful human being. Only through Balls of Steel was I able to get through this."

Of course there are days when I feel weak, for I still battle anxiety once in a while. But, I also can truthfully state how I've been through the worst and, thankfully, have come out the other side still intact. Many people have crumbled and failed on this journey. I didn't. The Balls of Steel metaphor will help you in other areas of your life as well. What if you get laid off from your job, or end up getting divorced? Knowing and believing that you have Balls of Steel will get you through those trials, just as well.

## HELPING OTHERS

Once you've recognized how successful you've been in coping with your loss, you can then begin thinking about helping others. I have found that if you try to help someone else who's also attempting to deal with a tragic loss, before you've gone through the grieving process yourself, you won't be able to do much good. It will be like one "sad sack" helping another "sad sack" without any positive results. This is the one time misery does NOT like or need company.

Once you're back on your own two feet, that's the time you can start thinking about helping others. You need to fix yourself first before even attempting to help anyone else. When you are ready to help others, it is a sign that you have successfully made the journey yourself, from the depths of despair to recovery as a functioning human being again.

# LETTERS AND POEMS TO SAMANTHA

# LETTER TO SAMANTHA

*February 17, 2007 9:30 a.m.*

*My dear, precious Samantha,*

*How I wish I could have saved you. I'm so sorry for not reacting to your cries sooner. Please forgive me, although I'm not sure how much of a difference it would have made.*

*I still can't believe you're gone, for I when I imagine you playing with Jakie and holding you in my arm, it seems so real to me, yet I know it's not.*

*I long to hear your laugh, see your smile and feel your sweet pats on my back. I miss everything about you, even changing your dirty diapers.*

*Like the Rabbi said at your funeral "You didn't know another life." In other words, we gave you a loving, supportive, fun life and I'm so thankful for those memories but, at the same time, they make me miss you to my core. My heart literally hurts when I think of you and all the amazing times we had together. I promise to always keep you alive in my heart and my soul.*

*You were such a special kid. Your "ear to ear" smile, so much like your mother's, could melt the hardest of hearts. People naturally gravitated toward you because you were so engaging, welcoming, cute and loving.*

*Your loss is such a painful blow. I'm feeling pain I never thought was humanly possible. You are loved so much and that's why the pain is felt so deeply.*

*I've often thought about switching places with you and would, in a second, if it weren't for Jakie and Mommy. I wish I could join you, if only so that I could hear you say "Dada" once again, but I know that wouldn't solve anything. In spite of my sorrow, I realize more than ever how precious life is and how I still have a lot to be thankful for... so I will go on.*

*Jakie misses you, too. You were his best friend and favorite playmate. Please send him some special sign to let him know how much you love and miss him, too, and that you want him to go on and be strong. He's been through so much, more than any little kid should ever have to endure. We're all so proud of him. Your big brother is a special child... but I don't need to tell you that. You knew that from day one, when he held you and fed you in the hospital.*

*I love viewing pictures of the two of you and how his smile widens as he looks lovingly at his baby sister and emits such limitless joy. A pure, beautiful site to see. I just hope to see that smile on him again and pray that he'll regain true happiness once more.*

*Mommy misses you too and still carries a heavy heart. After all, you were (are) her baby girl. There was such an unconditional love between you. Watching Mommy hold you and the special way you interacted with one another only confirmed that special bond and was an amazing sight to witness. With Mommy's devoted guidance, you were on your way to becoming an upstanding young lady.*

*It's devastating that you left us at such a young age. The saddest thing to watch was Mommy cleaning out your closet. While Mommy appears to be the strongest of us all and despite my hunger to have you back with us, I believe that she may yearn for you the most.*

*I told Jakie that his job is to make Mommy and Daddy laugh, and he's doing an A+ job at it. Remember how he was the only one who could make you laugh when you were crying? Well, now he's carried that skill over to us. He gives us tremendous joy. I don't know how Mommy and I could have endured this anguish or gone on with our lives (at least mine) without Jakie.*

*My love for Mommy and Jakie is what gets me through, but there will always be a huge hole in my heart caused by your absence and I now know the true meaning of the expression "I have a broken heart".*

*I've had a really hard time looking at your pictures. Seeing you exude such light and joy in those photos, juxtaposed with the images of your death, is just too much to handle. You know what I do sometimes, instead of looking at your pictures, I simply imagine you being here. And whenever Jakie and I are playing in the basement, I picture you there…actually "see" you playing with us. I can hear your voice and your laugh. It's like my own "virtual movie" and it makes me happy.*

*Maggie misses you, too. You guys truly loved one another. Just like Jakie, she lost her best friend. I'm trying to make her happy by playing with her, taking her for walks and giving her lots and lots of love. So, don't worry, my dear Samantha, your doggy is in good hands.*

*As I'm writing this letter, a song just came on the stereo called "Pick Myself Up" by Peter Tosh. I can't hear all the words but the chorus goes:*

**"I've got to pick myself up... dust myself off... and start all over again."**

*What perfect timing to hear this song because that's exactly what I need to do. Your Daddy's very sad, but I'll be okay. We'll all be okay.*

*I don't want to sign off because I want to keep talking to you. One thing that keeps me going is knowing that I have no regrets. I did all I could with you while you were here with us and I'm very thankful that I don't have to say "I wish I had spent more time with you", or "I wish I had told you that I love you more often." I did all that and more.*

*They say it's always harder on the ones left behind. Knowing how much you loved your family, I suspect it's just as hard on you, too. Have you looked at any of the photos I've left for you? I didn't want you to feel that you're alone. I wanted you to be able to look at them so that you would know that we're with you now...and always!*

*You're not alone, my Samantha...and neither are we.*

# POEM: SEARCHING FOR AN UNDERSTANDING

*April 17, 2009*

Tragedy
Why me, why you?
Choices
Where to go? What do we do now?
Lots of evil in the world today. Innocence. Pure joy.
We could use a little happiness and positive vibes.
Precious, innocent little girl giving pure joy to all.
Why can't we all enjoy and feel this? Don't we need more of
this? Why was it taken away?
Is there a God?
Little boy, little girl, children playing. Isn't this what life is
about?
Gone. Not right.
What could have been?
Searching for answers. Can anyone comprehend this?
No double tragedy. Don't lose your smile, Jake. You're my rock.
I love you more than anything.
Will this go away?
Love life
Be Strong and stay Strong
Face the future head on
Love
Live life
Balls of steel

# POEM: GETTING BETTER

*June 1, 2009*

In the clear?
Going forward? Not quite yet.
Missing, longing. Pain, pulling back
What to feel? Where to go? How to respond?
Overload? No.
Balls of steel
Stay focused
Responsibility
Jake, Robin, work, employees
Looking toward the future
Always in the past
Freedom? Never. Deep Connection
Comfort? Inner peace? Not now. Still fresh.
Future? Yes
Live and love life because it is precious and can be taken from
you in an instant
No fear.

www.ingramcontent.com/pod-product-compliance
Lightning Source LLC
Chambersburg PA
CBHW072020040426
42447CB00009B/1673